WHAT EVERY
CHRISTIAN
NEEDS
TO KNOW

WHAT EVERY CHRISTIAN NEEDS TO KNOW

GREG LAURIE

WHAT EVERY CHRISTIAN NEEDS TO KNOW

ISBN: 978-0-9843327-8-6

Published by: Kerygma Publishing—Allen David Books
Coordination: FM Management, Ltd.
Cover design: Highgate Cross+Cathey
Photography: Trever Hoehne
Editor: Highgate Cross+Cathey
Interior design: Highgate Cross+Cathey
Production: Highgate Cross+Cathey

24981 Dana Point Harbor Dr., Suite 110
Dana Point, CA 92629
www.kerygmapublishing.com

Printed in the United States of America

CONTENTS

PART ONE: THE BIBLE

PART TWO: PRAYER

PART THREE: SHARING THE GOOD NEWS

PART ONE
THE BIBLE

ONE
WHY READ THE BIBLE?

Let's talk about the Bible. You're a new believer. You've accepted Jesus as your Savior. Now you need some practical guidance that will help you live this new life.

You need to read the Bible.

Perhaps you've had one in your hands. You flipped it open, scanned some of the books, got really confused (perhaps you couldn't even understand some of the words, let alone the context), and put it aside as hopeless.

Maybe you've read a little bit. You began in Genesis and found it to be fairly interesting. Exodus was really good until about halfway through, and then you began to get a little stuck. But you persevered—that is, until you hit Leviticus and all bets were off.

So what's in this book called the Bible? Other Christians you know claim it's the most important book in their lives. If they're called upon to open to a certain book of the Bible—they can do it! They seem to comprehend what's going on.

Well, fear not. You can do the same. And this book will help you along the way.

GOD'S GIFT TO YOU

I can still remember the first time I started to read this incredible book, the Bible. I was able to find a very understandable translation and that made a big difference.

I soon discovered that this "user's manual" was the guide to life I had long been searching for. And it's available for you as well. Although the Bible continues to be the best-selling book of all time, it's also true that very few people actually sit down and read it. Even among Christians there is sometimes a disconnect. Many crack open their Bibles only on Sunday mornings at church, whereas the rest of the week it gathers dust on the nightstand.

Some people may avoid reading the Bible because they just don't know what to do with it. It doesn't make sense. It's unlike any other book they've read. It's divided up funny. It has weird language. It seems almost archaic at times. And yet it's very current. There's a single plot line and a central cast of characters. And what's really amazing is that it actually foretells the future.

But more about that later. First, to the issue at hand.

A *USA Today* survey of Americans revealed that more than 80 percent—including 71 percent of college graduates—believe the Bible is the inspired Word of God. Thirty-four percent believe the Bible is the actual Word of God, to be taken literally, word for word. However, the survey also revealed that people's beliefs about the Bible didn't necessarily correspond to their familiarity with what the Bible actually says.

For example, half of those who said they read the Bible regularly couldn't name any of the four Gospels of the New Testament. (The other 50 percent were able to name at least one.) Fewer than half knew who delivered the Sermon on the Mount. And even though 60 percent of Americans attend church on Easter Sunday, one-fourth didn't know what the occasion signifies! That's definitely a problem.

So we have the Bible at our fingertips, but many of us don't read it! Meanwhile, there are people all over the world who would give anything to have a copy of the Bible to read for themselves. In some countries, a church might have a single Bible—which they cut apart in order to pass the pages around to the people in the congregation. A person might receive a page to read for a while and then pass it along to someone else in time to get the next page.

A typical Christian bookstore in the United States has an overwhelming array of Bibles for sale. There are countless versions, with various types of study aids and other tools, and several different translations—not to mention the variety of bindings, from hardback to paperback to genuine or bonded leather.

Throw in all the different sizes and it can be mind-boggling!

Don't get me wrong. I think it's wonderful that we have so many choices. What's sad is to have such an abundance and yet squander it. We have so much available, yet so few people read and treasure God's Word.

I'm reminded of a true story I heard about a young man graduating from college. He hoped that his dad would give him a new car for a graduation present. Many of the other kids' fathers had given them new cars, and this boy wanted one, too. He had even picked out the one he wanted and told his father about it.

When graduation day finally arrived, the young man was shocked when his father handed him a brand new Bible instead of car keys. He was so outraged that he turned and walked away—leaving his father holding the Bible. The boy was so bitter that he cut off all contact with his father until the day his dad died.

Preparing for the funeral, the boy (now a man) went to his father's house to help get his affairs in order.

There, sitting on a shelf, was the Bible his father had given him for graduation. With tears in his eyes, he blew off the dust and opened it for the first time. Much to his amazement, he found an envelope with his name on it tucked inside the Bible. He opened it and found a cashier's check in the exact amount of the car he had picked out years ago.

In other words, his father had given him what he wanted, but he had to open the Bible to find out. Instead, he lost out on the car and a lifelong relationship with his father because he refused to open his Bible and discover the gift.

Sadly, that is essentially what we do when we never open the book that our heavenly Father has given us. Because inside this book is something far more valuable than a cashier's check.

THE USER'S MANUAL FOR LIFE

In the Bible we find words of life. In it is the truth about how to get to heaven. In it are the very words of God to us. What could be more valuable than that? Like any good instruction book, this "user's manual for life" tells us how to put it all together so that it works right. But if you're like me with most user's manuals, you're more likely to try out the gadget first, fiddle around with it, and read the directions later (and usually end up doing something the manual says you shouldn't do).

Some products come with a warning label. Some of these labels are helpful, and some are just plain silly. But most labels are probably there because somebody, somewhere, did something they shouldn't have done. Here are a few examples of warning labels I have read:

- On a cardboard windshield shade: "Warning. Don't drive with sun shield in place."

- On a hair dryer: "Don't use while sleeping."

- On an electric rotary tool: "This product is not intended for use as a dental drill."

- In the manual for a microwave oven: "Don't use for drying pets."

- On a child-size Superman costume: "Wearing of this garment does not enable you to fly."

Think of those poor people who tried to dry their hair while sleeping or tried to fly because they had on a cape. (And I don't even want to think about that microwave warning!) If only they had read the directions and warnings first! The same is true of life. The Bible gives us directions and warnings because God knows how sinful we are, how prone to fail and to get life all wrong.

The Bible has been used as a decoration on coffee tables, a booster seat for toddlers, a prop for preachers to wave in the air during a sermon, a place for witnesses to rest their left hand while taking an oath, or a convenient location to record the family tree.

But how often is the Bible read—and, most importantly, obeyed? Unfortunately, not often enough, even by Christians.

Don't make the same mistake!

The Bible isn't a Christian prop; it's God's direct message to you. Why read the Bible? Here are four good reasons:

1. *Studying the Bible is necessary for your spiritual growth.* The Bible tells you everything you need to know to grow in your new spiritual life.

2. *Studying the Bible keeps you spiritually strong.* The more you get into this book and apply its teachings, the more you will be able to stand your ground in the storms and trials of life.

3. *Studying the Bible gives you a "biblical worldview."* During these confused times of moral relativism, God desires that you make the Bible an integral part of your life.

4. *Studying the Bible helps you apply its truth to your life.* You will notice positive changes in your life as you apply what you read in Scripture.

Listen! Success or failure in your Christian life depends on how much of the Bible you get into your heart and mind on a daily basis, and how obedient you are to it. If you neglect to study the Scriptures, your spiritual life will ultimately unravel.

Everything you need to know about God is taught in the Bible.

A BOOK UNLIKE ALL OTHERS

The Bible is altogether different from any other book you'll ever read.

Take your favorite novel, for example. After you've read it once or twice, you're done. You might pick it up again a few years later just to refresh your memory about a familiar story or a style of writing that captured your imagination. But chances are you read it once and moved on to something else.

The Bible, however, isn't like that all.

It isn't like a book that you might read through once or twice and then return to the shelf to collect dust. The Bible is not a book that can be grasped completely in one reading—or a hundred—or a thousand. Why? Because the Bible is a *living* book.

> The word of God is living and active. Sharper than any double-edged sword, it penetrates even to dividing soul and spirit, joints and marrow; it judges the thoughts and attitudes of the heart. (Hebrews 4:12, NIV)

You can read the same Bible passage a hundred times in your lifetime, and the one-hundred-first time you may discover something you never noticed before, or you may learn a lesson that applies to your life right at that moment.

The Word of God isn't simply a collection of words from God, a vehicle for communicating ideas; it is living, life-changing, and dynamic as it works in us. With the incisiveness of a surgeon's knife, God's Word reveals who we are and what we are not. It penetrates the core of our moral and spiritual life. It discerns what is within us, both good and evil. The demands of God's Word require decisions. We must not only listen to the Word; we must also let it shape our lives.

That's why you want to keep reading it. Yet there's more to it than just reading along to feel good. You need to *study* the Bible in order to deepen your understanding and apply God's Word correctly. To make the most of your Bible study, you can read on your own and you can learn from others—pastors and teachers whose job it is to explain the Scriptures to you. You need to read the entire book so you can understand specific passages in their full context, and so you can understand the entire scope of God's revealed will in a particular area.

You need to understand the relationship of the Old Testament to the New Testament. In short, you need to become a disciple.

WHAT IT MEANS TO BE A DISCIPLE

The word disciple means "learner, a pupil, one who comes to be taught." However, the relationship is not merely that of a student listening passively to a lecturer.

A disciple listens attentively, with an intense desire to apply what is being taught, drinking in every word, marking every vocal inflection. We need inspired preaching and teaching, but we also need inspired listening!

Think of a pitcher and catcher in a baseball game. The catcher doesn't sit idly behind the plate, waiting for the pitch to hit his glove at speeds approaching one hundred miles per hour. If he did, he might get his head knocked off! Instead, he carefully watches each pitch and positions his glove and his body accordingly. The catcher is just as much a part of the game as the pitcher. The two are working together toward a common goal: striking out the batter.

As you sit in the pew on Sunday morning, the Holy Spirit is like the pitcher and you are like the catcher. The more attentive you are in listening to the Word of God, the greater the chances that each "pitch" will be a strike. You and the Holy Spirit share a common goal: that you will grow and flourish spiritually. It's all about learning how to listen!

This is why Jesus so often said, "Anyone who is willing to hear should listen and understand!" (Matthew 11:15; 13:9; 13:43, NLT).

Sometimes we listen more carefully than at other times. For example, how many times have you tuned out aboard an airplane while the flight attendant explained what to do in case of an emergency landing? How different would it be if you were flying across the Atlantic Ocean and the flight attendant announced that the plane was having engine trouble? All of a sudden, you'd be very interested in knowing that your seat cushion could be used as a flotation device.

Why? Because your life would depend on it!

In the same way, your spiritual life depends on studying God's Word. Simply listening to what Jesus teaches doesn't make anyone a true disciple. Only those who listen and obey what He says will be saved from destruction.

If you and I want to be true disciples of Jesus Christ, we must study the Word and apply what we read. As the apostle Paul said, "Don't be conformed to this world, but be transformed by the renewing of your mind, that you may prove what the will of God is, that which is good and acceptable and perfect" (Romans 12:2, NASB).

Here is a wonderful series of promises that will help us get the most from our study of Scripture:

> My child, listen to me and treasure my instructions. Tune your ears to wisdom, and concentrate on understanding. Cry out for insight and understanding. Search for them as you would for lost money or hidden treasure. Then you will understand what it means to fear the LORD, and you will gain knowledge of God. For the LORD grants wisdom! From his mouth come knowledge and understanding. He grants a treasure of good sense to the godly. He is their shield, protecting those who walk with integrity. He guards the paths of justice and protects those who are faithful to him. Then you will understand what is right, just, and fair, and you will know how to find the right course of action every time. (Proverbs 2:1-9, NLT)

Let's take a closer look at three key principles from this passage in Proverbs:

ONE: LISTEN TO GOD AND TREASURE HIS INSTRUCTIONS

First, you must see the intrinsic value of God's Word. This means you should be eager with anticipation when you open the Bible, asking, "What will God say to me today?" As you read, it's important to stop and think about what God might be showing you. Some people like to keep a journal where they can record thoughts, questions, prayers, and insights. This can be a helpful tool in your study.

Take your time and meditate on what you read. You don't need to read entire chapters or books at a time. Sometimes a few verses or paragraphs are all one can absorb. As you read, ask God to teach you how to treasure His Word.

TWO: CRY OUT FOR INSIGHT AND UNDERSTANDING

God doesn't expect you to understand everything you read right away. He knows this is all new to you. He lovingly offers to guide and teach you. His Holy Spirit will give you insight and understanding. Tell God you need His help. Cry out to Him for the insight and understanding you need to be able to learn and apply His words to your life.

THREE: SEEK WISDOM AS IF YOU WERE SEARCHING FOR LOST MONEY OR HIDDEN TREASURE

Want to attract a crowd? Drop a handful of change! Likewise, if you want to know God, He tells you to seek Him and His wisdom as though you were looking for lost money or digging for hidden treasure.

Listen! There is buried treasure in the Bible! But you can only find it when you search.

Proverbs 2:9 records an outstanding promise. Read it again:

> You will understand what is right, just, and fair, and you will know how to find the right course of action every time.

When you've listened to God and treasured His instructions, cried out for understanding, and sought His will in His word as if looking for treasure—guess what? You'll find the answers you need. You'll understand the right, just, and fair thing to do, and you'll know the right course of action every time! (NLT)

Jesus says, "If you continue in my word, you are truly my disciples" (John 8:31, NRSV). The word *continue* here is the same word he uses in John 15:7 where He speaks of "remaining" or "abiding" in His word:

"If you abide in me, and my words abide in you, ask for whatever you wish, and it will be done for you." (John 15:7, NRSV).

The word *abide* means to stay in a given place, to draw strength and resources from God. Picture a tree firmly planted in the ground. So we are to be planted in the Word.

Psalm 1 says that we should meditate on God's Word "day and night" (Psalm 1:2, NIV). If we are abiding in the Word, it means we're drawing our ideas and lifestyle from the Word, and what we say and do will be affected. Abiding in God's Word can transform your life. It will sustain you through the difficulties you face each day. It will help you with your thought life. It will guide you as you conduct yourself at school, at home, and even in your free time. It will help you make decisions. It will comfort you. It will challenge you. It will change you from the inside out.

It is only when you put yourself under the authority of God's Word and submit to its teaching that you become a growing disciple.

Colossians 3:16 (NRSV) says, "Let the word of Christ dwell in you richly." This literally means to "let the Word of Christ be perfectly at home in you."

God wants His Word to permeate every area of your life.

TWO
WHAT THE BIBLE SAYS ABOUT ITSELF

In the Bible, you will find a variety of words used to describe God's Word:

- command (or commands)

- commandments

- decrees

- laws

- precepts

- word (or words) of God

Don't be intimidated. Although a collection of laws, commands, and decrees might sound kind of dry to some, you'll soon discover that these precepts and principles often appear as part of exciting stories about people who obey or disobey God, in passionate speeches, or through amazing revelations.

You'll also discover that these commandments aren't "dry" at all, but like water to your thirsty soul or honey to your sweet tooth. For example, consider these verses from one of the beautiful songs found in the middle of your Bible in the collection called the Psalms:

The law of the LORD is perfect,
reviving the soul.

The decrees of the LORD are trustworthy,
making wise the simple.

The commandments of the LORD are right,
bringing joy to the heart.

The commands of the LORD are clear,
giving insight to life.

Reverence for the LORD is pure,
lasting forever.

The laws of the LORD are true;
each one is fair.

They are more desirable than gold,
even the finest gold.

They are sweeter than honey,
even honey dripping from the comb.

They are a warning to those who hear them;
there is great reward for those who obey them.
(Psalm 19:7-11, NLT)

THE WORD OF GOD IS PERFECT

This phrase "the law of the Lord" is a Hebrew term used to define the Scriptures. We are told "the law of the Lord is perfect." In other words, there is nothing to be added or taken away from it. The Bible says, "All Scripture is inspired by God and is useful to teach us what is true and to make us realize what is wrong in our lives. It straightens us out and teaches us to do what is right. It is God's way of preparing us in every way, fully equipped for every good thing God wants us to do" (2 Timothy 3:16-17, NLT).

The assertion that "all Scripture is inspired by God" literally means "all Scripture is God-breathed." In other words, the Bible is God's infallible Word. The first copies of the Scriptures (sometimes called by scholars the "original autographs") were without error. There are no mistakes, no contradictions; it is perfect.

Some recent discoveries, such as the Dead Sea Scrolls, have shown that the Bible we read today is still basically the same as what was written thousands of years ago!

The Bible is the only book you need to discover the foundational truths of how to know God and walk with Him. The Bible is your source for truth. As our society continues to change (almost always for the worse), you don't need to be blown about by the winds of change. You can stand on the firm foundation of God's Word. You can know what's right and what's wrong. Remember, the Bible is indeed the user's manual for life—a perfect manual with no mistakes.

THE WORD OF GOD TRANSFORMS

"The law of the LORD is perfect, reviving the soul" (Psalm 19:7, NLT).

Someone who says, "I'm not really interested in changing or being transformed" is probably not interested in the Bible. The truths found in the Bible will change your life. "For the word of God is full of living power. It is sharper than the sharpest knife, cutting deep into our innermost thoughts and desires. It exposes us for what we really are" (Hebrews 4:12, NLT).

If you have a sense of desperation about the circumstances of your life, you will find hope and peace. If you lack purpose in your life, you will discover that God created you for a purpose and that your life has meaning. If you're not sure where you came from or where you're going, you will find direction and guidance. If you have things in your life that you wish you could change, you will find that God has the power to make all things brand new:

- No longer do you need to be controlled by your passions.

- No longer will you be a mere victim of your circumstances.

- No longer must you cope alone with the pain in your life.

- No longer must you only wish that your relationships with others were better.

The Bible was written for people who don't have all the answers and who want something better. Even when you don't understand everything you read, even when you can't see the changes occurring in your life, it doesn't thwart God's purpose. Like a plant drawing minerals from the soil where it is planted, you are absorbing minerals of truth from the soil of God's Word.

The prophet Isaiah writes:

The rain and snow come down from the heavens and stay on the ground to water the earth. They cause the grain to grow, producing seed for the farmer and bread for the hungry. It is the same with my word. I send it out, and it always produces fruit. It will accomplish all I want it to, and it will prosper everywhere I send it. (Isaiah 55:10-11, NLT)

If you're struggling with your attempts to read the Bible, don't be discouraged. Maybe you don't know exactly what's going on or why something is happening or who the prophet Isaiah is, but keep reading.

God promises that His Word "always produces fruit." You may not understand all about minerals and how they go from the soil to the plant—all you know is that a plant dies if it isn't rooted in the ground. Take up those minerals and let God provide the growth in you.

As you keep reading, attending church, and learning, pretty soon the pieces will begin to come together and make more and more sense. And God will keep His Word working in your life—even when you don't understand it all. Slowly but surely it will work a transformation in your life. Watch and see!

THE WORD OF GOD GIVES WISDOM

"The decrees of the Lord are trustworthy, making wise the simple"
(Psalm 19:7, NLT).

The Hebrew word translated simple comes from a root that speaks of an open door. The "simple" person, then, has a mind like an open door—everything comes in and goes out. This person does not know what to keep in or keep out. He is totally naive, open to everything, closed to nothing. The Bible says it is able to make such a person wise!

I wasn't raised in a Christian home. When I was in my teens and asked the Lord to come into my life, I began to read the Bible for the first time. I was amazed at how completely relevant it was to my life. At times I was surprised to find the ink was dry on its pages because it seemed as if it had been written just for me only moments before:

- When I needed to know about relationships, I found a lot of examples in the Bible—good examples, bad examples, and wise counsel about how to be a good friend, spouse, boss, and employee.

- When I needed to know about marriage, I discovered that the Bible has a lot to say about that, too.

- When I wanted to know how to live life to its fullest, I found that the Bible answered my questions.

- When I wanted to learn how to be wise, I knew I'd come to the right place.

How can one book do all that? Remember Isaiah's prophecy quoted above: God will make His Word produce fruit in your life. Sometimes one verse will stand out to you and give you direction in a particular situation. Sometimes the story of a person's struggles will give you insight into how to (or how not to) act in your own life. You gain wisdom because you're following God's directions. You're learning how to become wise.

THE WORD OF GOD IS RIGHT

"The commandments of the LORD are right" (Psalm 19:8, NLT).

In Hebrew, this declaration means that the Bible has set out the right path for you to follow. The Bible teaches you right and wrong in your life.

Take another look at 2 Timothy 3:16-17 (NLT): "All Scripture is inspired by God and is useful to teach us what is true and to make us realize what is wrong in our lives. It straightens us out and teaches us to do what is right. It is God's way of preparing us in every way, fully equipped for every good thing God wants us to do."

This is why it's so essential to read the Word of God. Consider this promise to those who will do what the Lord wants:

Oh, the joys of those
who do not follow the advice of the wicked,
or stand around with sinners,
or join in with scoffers.

But they delight in doing everything the LORD wants;
day and night they think about his law.
They are like trees planted along the riverbank,
bearing fruit each season without fail.
Their leaves never wither,
and in all they do, they prosper.

But this is not true of the wicked.
They are like worthless chaff, scattered by the wind.
They will be condemned at the time of judgment.
Sinners will have no place among the godly.

For the LORD watches over the path of the godly,
but the path of the wicked leads to destruction.
(Psalm 1:1-6, NLT)

Psalm 119:9 (NLT) says, "How can a young person stay pure? By obeying your word and following its rules." The apostle Paul writes to his young friend Timothy: "Work hard so God can approve you. Be a good worker, one who does not need to be ashamed and who correctly explains the word of truth" (2 Timothy 2:15, NLT).

To know God, you must first know His Word. I heard the story of an old recluse who lived deep in the mountains of Colorado. When he died, some of his distant relatives came from the city to collect his valuables. Upon arriving, all they found was an old shack with an outhouse beside it. Inside the shack, next to the rock fireplace, was an old cooking pot and some mining equipment.

A cracked table with a three-legged chair stood guard by a tiny window, and an old kerosene lamp served as the centerpiece for the table. In the dark corner of the little room was a dilapidated cot with a bedroll on it. Deciding there wasn't anything there of value, the family members left.

As they were driving away, an old friend of the recluse flagged them down. "Y'all mind if I help myself to what's left in my friend's cabin?" he asked.

"Go right ahead," they replied. After all, they thought, nothing inside the shack was worth anything.

The old friend entered the shack and walked directly over to the table. He reached underneath and lifted up one of the floorboards, then proceeded to take out all the gold his friend had discovered in the past fifty-three years—it was worth millions! Apparently the recluse had died with only his close friend knowing his true worth.

As the friend looked out the little window and watched the disappearing cloud of dust behind the family members' car, he said, "They shoulda got to know him better!"

The same is true with us and our friend Jesus Christ. So many Christians behave like distant relatives, even though Jesus has invited us to intimate friendship.

Jesus has many wonderful treasures to reveal to you from His Word. Those treasures will set you on the pathway to a completely fulfilling life, for you will be doing exactly what God has prepared for you to do.

His Word is right, and it shows the right way for you to go.

THE WORD OF GOD BRINGS HAPPINESS

The Word of God brings "joy to the heart" (Psalm 19:8, NLT).

If you want peace, joy, meaning, and purpose in life, you've come to the right place. Jesus said, "Blessed…are those who hear the word of God and obey it" (Luke 11:28, NIV).

Perhaps you're looking at your Bible, with all its small print and confusing words, and the prospect of reading it doesn't make you very happy or joyful.

Trust me. Dig in. Search for the treasure. Let God make it work in your life. You'll discover that the Bible is indeed "more desirable than gold" and "sweeter than honey, even honey dripping from the comb."

God gives you a promise. Not only does He set His Word to work in your life, but He adds that "there is great reward for those who obey" His Word. Jesus said to the Jews who believed Him, "You are truly my disciples if you keep obeying my teachings. And you will know the truth, and the truth will set you free" (John 8:31-32, NLT). Now that's happiness!

THREE
HOW YOU CAN KNOW THE BIBLE IS TRUE

You may be saying to yourself, "That's all well and good what the Bible says about itself. But I can say a lot of things about myself, too, and that doesn't make them true!"

That's a fair statement. After all, if you're going to stake your life on something, you need to know it's worth that kind of commitment.

Let's talk about how you can know that the Bible is true. I am indebted to my friend John MacArthur for the following outline on the truthfulness of Scripture.

ONE: I KNOW THE BIBLE IS TRUE BECAUSE IT IS CONFIRMED BY MY EXPERIENCE.

Personal experience isn't the only reason I believe in the truth of Scripture, and it's perhaps not the most convincing evidence to skeptics, but it has certainly helped me to believe. For example, the Bible says that God will forgive my sins:

> If we confess our sins to him, he is faithful and just to forgive us and to cleanse us from every wrong. (1 John 1:9, NLT)

One day I chose to believe that. I accepted God's forgiveness—and you know what? The sense of guilt and the heavy burden I had been carrying was taken away.

The Bible also says that if I come to Jesus, I will become a different person:

> Those who become Christians become new persons. They are not the same anymore, for the old life is gone. A new life has begun! (2 Corinthians 5:17, NLT)

I trusted my life to Jesus and I've been transformed. I'm still a "work in progress," of course, but the change has happened. The Bible says that God will give me His peace and joy if I trust Christ:

> "I am leaving you with a gift—peace of mind and heart. And the peace I give isn't like the peace the world gives. So don't be troubled or afraid....You haven't done this before. Ask, using my name, and you will receive, and you will have abundant joy" (John 14:27; 16:24, NLT).

Since I became a Christian, I have experienced times of wonderful peace and incredible joy—just as He promised.

The Bible says that God will answer my prayers (if I pray properly):

> "If you believe, you will receive whatever you ask for in prayer." (Matthew 21:22, NLT)

I believe what the Bible says, and my prayers have been answered. If you read the Bible, you will discover it is full of promises made to God's people—which now includes you. As you live your new Christian life, you will find the truth of God's Word borne out in your daily experience.

TWO: I KNOW THE BIBLE IS TRUE BECAUSE IT IS CONFIRMED BY SCIENCE.

You might be thinking, "No, the Bible and science contradict each other." That's not necessarily true. There are many who have scoffed at the Bible, saying how unscientific it is. Yet it was the Bible that first said that the number of the stars is beyond counting. Scripture says that God "stretched forth the heavens" (Isaiah 51:13, KJV) into a limitless expanse which can never be measured and filled it with "countless millions" of stars (Genesis 22:17).

To the average observer looking into the sky with the latest telescope technology, the visible stars aren't uncountable. There are a vast number, but they don't seem impossible to count. Yet the Bible flatly states that the number of the stars can be compared, literally, to the number of the grains of sand upon the seashore.

Modern science has now established this to be true. People can't possibly begin to assess the number of the stars.

The Bible also says that God "suspends the earth over nothing" (Job 26:7, NIV). In that poetic way it describes the mysterious force of gravity, which no one even yet understands but which keeps the earth suspended in its relationship to the sun and the other planets. As the Bible says, the earth literally hangs upon nothing.

The Bible says, "Things which are seen were not made of things which do appear" (Hebrews 11:3, KJV), thus predating by many centuries the discoveries of modern science that finally recognized that all matter is made up of invisible energy and that matter and energy are interchangeable.

I don't believe in the Bible because science proves that it's true; rather, I believe in the science that the Bible proves is true.

Having said all that, let me point out something that is very important for us to understand about the Bible. *It is not the Bible's purpose to be a textbook on science*. If it were, the book would be much thicker than it is, and probably much less comprehensible. Rather, the Bible is intended to be a book of redemption. Its primary purpose is not to tell us how the heavens go, but how to go to heaven. It tells us how to know

God and how to live as part of this troubled and confused human race. It is the only book that speaks with authority in this realm.

THREE: I KNOW THE BIBLE IS TRUE BECAUSE IT IS CONFIRMED BY ARCHAEOLOGY.

Over the years, countless critics have challenged the teachings of the Bible. But recent archaeological findings have confirmed Scripture's teachings time and time again.

For years, many skeptics doubted that crucifixion took place at all. Contrary to Scripture, they contended that Jesus dying on a cross never happened. You can see how such criticism strikes at the very heart of our faith. But these contrary voices were silenced in 1968 when the remains of a crucified man were discovered north of Jerusalem. The skeleton had a seven inch iron nail still embedded in the heel, and the state of the bones indicated that his arms had been outstretched.

Once again, the Bible gave the information before the "experts" had it. Others doubted the Bible because they could find no historical record of a Roman governor named Pontius Pilate. But in 1961 an inscription found at Caesarea Maritima confirmed that Pontius Pilate was the Roman governor in Judea at the time of Jesus' crucifixion.

Some doubted Scripture's authority because no record of a high priest named Caiaphas existed. But in 1990, Caiaphas's tomb was discovered.

A number of years ago, some archaeologists claimed to have found Noah's ark. On September 25, 2000, *U.S. News & World Report* published a story about some archaeologists, led by oceanographer Robert Ballard (who found the Titanic), who have been searching beneath the Black Sea off the Turkish coast for evidence of an apocalyptic natural event that could have inspired the Genesis account of the great flood. The expedition found a large wooden building twelve miles offshore at a depth of more than three hundred feet. The explorers also found ample evidence of a widespread flood, just a the Bible says.

Could this wooden structure be Noah's ark? I don't know, but in any case, I don't believe the Bible is true because archaeology confirms it. I believe archaeology is true because the Bible confirms it.

FOUR: I KNOW THE BIBLE IS TRUE BECAUSE IT IS CONFIRMED BY ITS MANY PROPHECIES THAT HAVE COME TRUE.

When we talk about Bible prophecies, we don't mean tabloid predictions; we're referring to very specific prophecies that have been fulfilled over a span of hundreds of years. No other religion has prophets who predict the future with such uncanny accuracy as the prophets in the Bible.

Why not? If they were to attempt it, it would soon be evident that they aren't inspired by God. God can speak of the future with absolute certainty because He knows it as well as we know the past.

The basic test of true prophets—and by extension the one true God and the one true faith—is this: Can they predict the future without error? The Bible is full of stories about prophets who predicted future events, not just once or twice, but hundreds of times! And many more prophecies have yet to be fulfilled—but they will be.

It's worth noting that two-thirds of the Bible consists of prophecy. One-half of these prophecies have already been fulfilled. If half of the prophecies have already come true just as the Bible said, should I have any reason to doubt that the remaining ones will happen exactly as God has promised? When God says something is going to happen, you can take it to the bank.

A college professor asked his class to estimate the odds of having eight prophecies fulfilled by one man:

- The odds that he would be born in Bethlehem (predicted in Micah 5:2, fulfilled in Matthew 2:1): 1 in 280,000.

- The odds that a forerunner would announce his coming (predicted in Malachi 3:1, fulfilled in Luke 3:4): 1 in 1,000.

- The odds that he would ride into Jerusalem on a donkey (predicted in Zechariah 9:9, fulfilled in Matthew 21:1-10): 1 in 1,000.

- The odds that he would be betrayed by a friend and his hands and feet would be pierced (predicted in Psalm 22:16; Zechariah 13:6, fulfilled in Luke 23:33): 1 in 1,000.

- The odds that he would be betrayed for thirty pieces of silver (predicted in Zechariah 11:12, fulfilled in Matthew 26:14-16): 1 in 10,000.

- The odds that the one who betrayed him would throw the thirty pieces of silver down in the temple and that the money would be used to purchase a potter's field (predicted in Zechariah 11:13, fulfilled in Matthew 27:5-7): 1 in 100,000.

- The odds that he would offer no defense when placed on trial for his life (predicted in Isaiah 53:7, fulfilled in Matthew 26:62-63; Mark 14:60-61): 1 in 10,000.

- The odds that he would be executed by crucifixion (predicted in Psalm 22:16, fulfilled in Luke 23:32-33): 1 in 10,000.

If you put all these together and divide by the total number of people who have lived since the time of these prophecies, the odds that all eight prophecies would be fulfilled by one person, Jesus Christ, is 1^{10}. (That's a one followed by twenty-one zeroes!)

Here's another way to look at it: If you were to cover the entire landmass of the earth with silver dollars 120 feet deep, mark one of the coins, and then blindfold someone and ask him to walk around the world and randomly reach down and pick the one that was marked, he would have as much of a chance of choosing the right coin as Jesus had of fulfilling those eight prophecies. And yet, Jesus not only fulfilled the eight prophecies I mentioned, He also fulfilled many others.

Despite this compelling evidence, the accuracy of the Bible—and the truth about Jesus—is continually under attack in our society.

There will always be critics who want to point their finger at the Bible and question its authenticity. There will be groups who will try to cut it apart, saying this part is true and that part isn't. Ultimately, the issue of the Bible comes down to faith.

As you establish a habit of reading your Bible, you will discover that you won't be able to explain everything you read. That's okay. You see, the Bible isn't meant to be a scientific textbook. Instead, it is the story of salvation. It explains the basic problem with humanity (our sin), the trouble we get into as a result of sin, and God's solution to our problem—sending Jesus to die on our behalf, to pay the price for our sin, and to break its power in our lives.

Essentially, that's it. From Genesis to Revelation, the Bible is one long story with a common theme. Dr. W. A. Criswell, the late pastor of First Baptist Church in Dallas, used to call it "the scarlet thread of redemption."

Technically speaking, the Bible isn't one book; it's actually sixty-six books written over a 1,500-year span. It was written by more than forty authors from every walk of life, including kings, peasants, philosophers, fishermen, poets, statesmen, and scholars. Writers include Moses, a political leader trained in the universities of Egypt; Peter, a fisherman; Joshua, a military general; Daniel, a prime minister; Luke, a doctor; Solomon, a king; Matthew, a tax collector; Paul, a rabbi.

The Bible was written in different places. Moses and David often wrote in the wilderness; Jeremiah, in a dungeon; Daniel, on a hillside and in a palace; Paul, inside prison walls; Luke, while traveling, often by ship.

Each one of these men was inspired by God to write their words. God used these different writers—with their personal perspectives and even the different audiences to whom they wrote—and inspired their writing so that it is, literally, God's words.

In spite of great diversity of authorship in the Old Testament (OT) and New Testament (NT), and composition spanning over 1,500 years, there is remarkable unity in the total thrust.

Christians believe that God must have been superintending the production of a divine-human book that would properly present His message to humankind.

The OT and NT are component parts of one divine revelation. The OT describes man and woman in the first paradise on the old earth; the NT concludes with a vision of the new heaven and the new earth. The OT sees humankind as fallen from a sinless condition and separated from God; the NT views believers as restored to favor through the sacrifice of Christ. The OT predicts a coming Redeemer who will rescue men and women from eternal condemnation; the NT reveals the Christ who brought salvation. In most of the OT the spotlight focuses on a sacrificial system in which the blood of animals provided a temporary handling of the sin problem; in the New, Christ appeared as the one who came to put an end to all sacrifice—to be himself the supreme sacrifice. In the OT, numerous predictions foretold a coming Messiah who would save his people; in the New, scores of passages detail how those prophecies were minutely fulfilled in the person of Jesus Christ.

As Augustine said more than 1,500 years ago, "The New is in the Old contained; the Old is in the New explained."

The following quote explains what Christians mean when we talk about the Bible being "inspired" by God.

The Bible is not a collection of stories, fables, myths, or merely human ideas about God. It is not a human book. Through the Holy Spirit, God revealed his person and plan to certain believers, who wrote down his message for his people (2 Peter 1:20-21). This process is known as inspiration. The writers wrote from their own personal, historical, and cultural contexts. Although they used their own minds, talents, language, and style, they wrote what God wanted them to write. Scripture is completely trustworthy because God was in control of its writing. Its words are entirely authoritative for our faith and lives. The Bible is "God-breathed." Read it, and use its teachings to guide your conduct.[1]

All these different people, across a span of centuries, wrote a book that ultimately tells one story: why people need to be saved and how God provided for salvation. The complexity and cohesiveness of the Bible couldn't "just happen." Only God, through His Holy Spirit, working through human writers, could have developed this incredible book—God's true and everlasting words to you.

FOUR
HOW TO STUDY THE BIBLE

I f I have convinced you that it's important to get into God's Word so that God's Word can get into you—great!

But now what?

Well, let's dig in.

GETTING STARTED ON BIBLE STUDY
GET A BIBLE

You may already have a Bible. However, if it's an older translation, you may find that the language is a little difficult to read and understand. Fortunately, Christian translators have worked hard to continually update the Bible's language, making it easier to read and understand.

So…if you have a King James Version and you can't understand very much that it says—don't worry. Take a trip to your local Christian bookstore. You'll be amazed to discover the variety of translations and study Bibles that are now available. (For help in wading through your many options, see the section at the end of this chapter called "Choosing a Bible.")

SET ASIDE SOME QUIET TIME

You've probably heard other Christians talk about having their "quiet time" or their "devotions." They are referring to their own private Bible reading and prayer time. All believers need to set aside time every day to read their Bibles and pray. Sadly, many Christians don't do this—to their own detriment.

This is a time when you and God can talk. It's your opportunity to sit down with someone who loves you very much and who wants to guide you through the day ahead. Why would you miss that appointment?

Look at your schedule and set aside at least a few minutes every day to study God's Word and pray. There's no right or wrong way to do this—just find a time that works for you. Maybe you need to get up a bit earlier, when the house is quiet and you won't be interrupted. Maybe you can do it over lunch. Perhaps the best time for you will be right before you go to bed. The point is to schedule a time so that it becomes a habit to spend time with God.

This may be one of the biggest changes you'll see in your life—this scheduled time to read the Bible and pray. But it's this very important habit that will provide the foundation for your Christian life. As I've noted in previous chapters, you need God's Word, and the only way to get it is to spend time reading it every day.

PRAY FOR WISDOM AND UNDERSTANDING

The most often overlooked and undervalued aspect of Bible study is prayer. Prayer is essential to gaining wisdom and understanding when you read God's Word. Through prayer, you can approach God and acknowledge your incomplete knowledge of His Word, as well as your need for Him to open your heart to His instruction. Therefore, determine to begin each study with prayer. Only God can give you the wisdom to understand His Word.

Here's a simple prayer you can pray: *Lord, I'm new to Bible study and prayer—yet I understand how important they are for me to grow spiritually. As I open Your Word today, teach me something that will help me through my day.*

READ IN AN ORDERLY MANNER

If you received a letter and read only a few sentences here and there, the letter would not make much sense to you. But if you read the letter from beginning to end, you would understand it. The same holds true when you read the Bible.

This is where a lot of people get off track in their study of the Bible. They adopt a "hunt and peck" method—a little bit from Genesis… throw in a few verses from Matthew…take a quick dash through Jude…and top it off with a heavy dose of Revelation.

The result, as you might expect, is spiritual indigestion!

One danger of taking a haphazard approach to reading the Bible is that we might be tempted to isolate passages and take them out of context. (This is done regularly in many cult groups.) For instance, let's take a look at Philippians 2:12:

> Therefore, my beloved, as you have always obeyed, not as in my presence only, but now much more in my absence, work out your own salvation with fear and trembling.

Some have used this verse to say, "You have to work for your salvation." But if you read the following verse, Philippians 2:13, you gain some valuable perspective:

> For it is God who works in you both to will and to do for His good pleasure.

Context is very important in understanding and interpreting Scripture. It's also important to consider other verses that speak to the same subject. For example, Ephesians 2:8-9 (NIV) gives us more information about whether we need to work for our salvation:

> For it is by grace you have been saved, through faith— and this not from yourselves, it is the gift of God—not by works, so that no one can boast.

You can see why a thorough and systematic study of the Bible is so important if we want to understand God's message to us. It doesn't necessarily mean that you have to read straight through from Genesis to Revelation. Work on one book at a time, but keep going until you have finished the entire Bible. It might be easier to begin in the New Testament, perhaps with the Gospel of John. This book was written to help us see that Jesus is the Son of God. After you have finished reading John, read the rest of the New Testament.

Once you have finished the New Testament, which covers the life of Jesus on earth and the establishment of the early church, start reading the Old Testament, which tells the story of the nation of Israel and foreshadows the coming of Jesus the Messiah.

Make it your goal to read the whole Bible—but not before next Sunday. Take your time, and read thoroughly. At the end of this book is a reading plan to help you read through the entire New Testament in a year. There are other reading plans available that will help you read through the entire Bible in a year.

Every book in the Bible is included for a reason. Reading everything will help you become familiar with the "whole counsel of God."

FINISH WHAT YOU START

In life, the benefits of doing anything are often not realized until the task is completed. The same is true of reading a book from the Bible.

Once you've chosen a book to read, read it from beginning to end. Although you may benefit spiritually by reading a verse from one book or a story from another, you will profit more by reading the entire book because it puts each verse and story in its proper context. Thus, you will have a better understanding of what it means. In addition, by reading books from beginning to end, you will become more familiar with the Bible as a whole. You may even discover passages that will one day become your favorites.

MEDITATE ON GOD'S WORD AND ASK QUESTIONS

I can't overemphasize the importance of taking time to think about what you have read. As you meditate on God's Word, He will help you discover the importance of each passage of Scripture. It will also help you examine your life in light of what God has revealed in His Word.

When I use the word "meditate," I'm not referring to transcendental meditation or the New Age practice of emptying your mind. The biblical idea of meditation means to "chew something over," to contemplate or consider.

One of the best ways to begin meditating on God's Word is to ask questions. Here are a few questions to help you get started:

- What is the main subject of the passage?

- To whom is the passage addressed?

- Who is speaking?

- About what or whom is the person speaking?

Take a couple of minutes to think about each passage you read. If you read a whole chapter, you might need to break it down into paragraphs to help you in your understanding. Then, for each section, ask these two questions:

- What is the key verse?

- What does this passage teach me about God?

Next, to see how the text might apply to you personally, ask yourself these questions:

- Is there any sin mentioned in the passage that I need to confess or forsake?

- Is there a command given that I should obey?

- Is there a promise made that I can apply to my current circumstances?

- Is there a prayer given that I could pray?

INVEST IN A FEW GOOD RESOURCE BOOKS

The Bible alludes to many ancient customs that are completely unfamiliar to us today. Much of the subtle meaning behind these allusions that would give us greater insight into and appreciation for God's Word is therefore lost. To understand the culture in which the Bible was written, you may want to purchase a few good biblical resource books.

There are two types of books you should consider purchasing: a one- or two-volume commentary on the whole Bible, and a Bible dictionary. Most one-or-two-volume commentaries are concise. They give you the necessary information on important words, phrases, and verses from the Bible. They won't comment on every verse, and they won't give a detailed explanation of any one verse, but they're good resources to help you begin to understand God's Word.

Bible dictionaries contain short articles (in alphabetical order) on people, places, and objects found in the Bible. Some Bible dictionaries also contain maps, diagrams, and pictures of cities, regions, and artifacts.

Here's a short list of resources that you may find helpful in your study of the Bible: *Life Application New Testament Commentary; Halley's Bible Handbook; the "Be" series of commentaries by Warren Wiersbe; New Believer's Bible; Tyndale Bible Dictionary.*

I have done extensive teaching on Old and New Testament books, and these messages are available on CD and audio cassette. For more information, log on to www.harvest.org

CHOOSING A BIBLE
WHAT ABOUT ALL THESE BIBLE TRANSLATIONS?

If you're in the market for a Bible, you might find yourself confused by the huge variety available. Various publishers have done lots of hard work to help make the Bible understandable and helpful. In this section, I've listed some of the most common Bible versions you will find at most Christian bookstores or your favorite online book outlet. I've also included a brief overview of each version.

The original texts of the Bible were written in Hebrew (Old Testament) and Greek (New Testament). Later some Jewish scholars translated the Hebrew Old Testament into Greek because Greek was the everyday language of much of the world, beginning about two hundred years before the time of Christ.

Eventually the entire text of the Bible was translated into Latin. Unfortunately, as the influence of the Roman Empire waned, soon only priests and scholars, who had been trained in the classical languages, could read the Latin Scriptures.

In Great Britain, William Tyndale (1484–1536), who is known as "The Father of the English Bible," wanted to translate the Bible into English so the common people could read it. However, he could not get permission from the government, so he went to Germany and was able to publish an English translation of the New Testament in 1526. By 1530, he had completed the first five books of the Old Testament (Genesis, Exodus, Leviticus, Numbers, and Deuteronomy—also called the Pentateuch).

However, he was later found guilty of heresy because of his translation work and was burned at the stake in 1536. Since then, the Bible has been translated into hundreds of languages, and dozens of English translations are available. Here's a brief overview of the major translations currently available:

KING JAMES VERSION (KJV), NEW KING JAMES VERSION (NKJV)

William Tyndale's work formed the foundation for what would eventually be the most significant English Bible translation ever completed—what came to be called the King James Version, published in 1611. This version was prepared at the request of King James I of England and became the standard English version of the Bible for three centuries. In fact, you can still purchase the King James Version. Many people still prefer it for the eloquence of its language. I was raised studying the King James Version and still love and value it.

The KJV includes archaic pronouns like "thee" and "thou" and may be a bit difficult to read. However, you can also find a version called the New King James Version, published in 1982, which replaces much of the archaic language with more current terms.

REVISED STANDARD VERSION (RSV); NEW REVISED STANDARD VERSION (NRSV)

These translations are exactly what the name suggests: revisions of earlier texts. As language evolves, many Bible translations are updated accordingly. In 1952, the American Standard Version, an earlier translation of the Bible, was updated and revised. The result was the Revised Standard Version. Today you will also find the New Revised Standard Version, which was published in 1990 to update the RSV.

NEW AMERICAN STANDARD BIBLE (NASB)

The NASB is another revision of the American Standard Version, this one published by the Lockman Foundation in 1971. The translators of this version attempted to adhere to the style and syntax of the original languages while creating an easily readable English version.

NEW INTERNATIONAL VERSION (NIV)

The New International Version is a completely new rendering of the original languages done by a group of international scholars (hence the "international" in the title). They worked to provide a thought-for-thought translation in contemporary English. They were working to find a point midway between a literal rendering (such as in the NASB) and a more free-flowing translation. They wanted to pass along, in readable English, the thoughts of the original writers. The complete NIV was first published in 1978, was revised and updated in 1984, and is still in wide use today.

NEW CENTURY VERSION (NCV)

Another translation from the original languages is available in an edition called The Everyday Bible. First published in 1993, the NCV emphasizes simplicity and clarity. It was meant to be easy even for children to read, so the translators used short sentences and third-grade level vocabulary.

CONTEMPORARY ENGLISH VERSION (CEV)

The CEV takes technical terms such as "salvation," "grace," and "righteousness" (words that may not be clearly understood by many readers) and changes them to natural English equivalents such as "God saves you," "God is kind to you," and "God accepts you." This contemporary version was completed in 1994.

NEW LIVING TRANSLATION (NLT)

In 1971, Dr. Kenneth Taylor, founder of Tyndale House Publishers, completed a paraphrase of the entire Bible, which Tyndale published as The Living Bible. Later, this popular version was completely revised to create the New Living Translation. More than ninety evangelical scholars and theologians undertook the seven-year-long task of completing the NLT. The NLT remains true to the readability of The Living Bible yet is close to the Hebrew and Greek texts in meaning as well as style. The NLT was first published in 1996.

Perhaps the best way to choose the version that is right for you is simply to read the same passages in different versions and see which one appeals to you the most. I primarily use the New King James Version and the New Living Translation, although I incorporate many other translations in my study as well.

Even though the wording from one translation to another is slightly different, always remember that God protects His Word. The message is the same and it is still God's inspired Word. We can thank God for people like William Tyndale, who labored to bring the Word of God into English (and, in his case, gave his life for it), and for translators today who labor to make God's Word readable and accessible in hundreds of languages.

FIVE
OVERVIEW OF THE BIBLE

The Bible is God's story of our salvation. It explains our basic problem (sin) and the solution that God has provided (sending Jesus to die on our behalf). If you keep the basic story in mind as you read, it will help you understand much of what God is saying through His Word.

At the end of this chapter, you will find a summary of each book of the Bible, including its author, the date it was written, the genre (or type of literature) it is, and a short summary of what the book contains.

Let's take a journey through the Bible!

The Bible is divided into the Old Testament and the New Testament. Of course, there was no OT and NT before the coming of Christ, only one collection of sacred writings. But after the apostles and their associates produced another body of sacred literature, the church began to refer to the OT and NT.

Actually "testament" is the Greek word that might better be rendered "covenant." It denotes an arrangement made by God for the spiritual guidance and benefit of human beings. The covenant is unalterable: humankind may accept it or reject it but cannot change it.

At least the first half of the OT follows a logical and easily understood arrangement. In Genesis through Esther the history of Israel from Abraham to the restoration [of Israel] appears largely in chronological order. Then follows a group of poetic books and the Major and Minor prophets ("Major" meaning the books that are relatively long; "Minor" meaning the books that are relatively short).

The NT also follows a generally logical arrangement. It begins with the four Gospels, which describe the birth, life, death, and resurrection of Christ and his training of disciples to carry on His work after His ascension. The book of Acts continues the narrative where the Gospels end and details the founding of the church and its spread lands. In the latter part of the book the spotlight focuses on the apostle Paul and his church planting activities. Next come letters Paul addressed to churches he founded or to young ministers he tried to encourage. Following the Pauline epistles come a group commonly called the General Epistles [by other authors, such as Peter, James, and John]. The last book, Revelation, is an apocalyptic work. Revelation (literally "the unveiling") unlocks the "last days" scenario for us. It also is the only book of the Bible with a special blessing attached to the person who reads and keeps its words.

THE OLD TESTAMENT
GENESIS

Writer: Moses
Date: 1450–1410 B.C.
Literary Style: Narrative
Genesis is the first book of the Bible. The word genesis means

"the origin or coming into being of something." Recorded here are such important beginnings as the Creation, the fall of man, and the early years of the nation of Israel. Familiar stories about people such as Abraham, Isaac, Jacob, and Joseph are all found in this book.

EXODUS

Writer: Moses
Date: 1450–1410 B.C.
Literary Style: Narrative

Exodus is about deliverance. The Israelites have moved to Egypt because of a famine. While there, they are made slaves. Because the Israelites are God's people, He appoints Moses to lead the Israelites out of Egypt and to the Promised Land, Canaan. On the way there, the Israelites stop at Mount Sinai, where God gives them the Ten Commandments.

LEVITICUS

Writer: Moses
Date: 1445–1444 B.C.
Literary Style: Law

Leviticus deals with the worship of a holy God. Here God gives the priests and people rules to live by to present themselves as holy before Him.

NUMBERS

Writer: Moses
Date: 1450–1410 B.C.
Literary Style: Narrative

Numbers takes its name from the two censuses (or "numberings") of the people recorded in this book. Yet Numbers is actually a sequel to Exodus. It follows the wanderings of the Israelites through the wilderness of Sinai for the next forty years until they camp just east of the Promised Land.

DEUTERONOMY

Writer: Moses
Date: 1407–1406 B.C.
Literary Style: Narrative

Deuteronomy is a farewell speech given to the people of Israel by Moses, just before his death. Moses knows that the people will face many new temptations as they move into the Promised Land. He knows they need to be reminded of God's promises to them and their responsibility to God and His laws.

JOSHUA

Writer: Joshua and possibly Phinehas
Date: Unknown
Literary Style: Narrative

Joshua is a book of conquest. Here the Israelites finally take possession of the Promised Land. The conquest is not immediate, though. It is a process of faith and action, through which God displays His miraculous power.

JUDGES

Writer: Probably Samuel
Date: Unknown
Literary Style: Narrative

This is a book about backsliding, defeat, and God's gracious deliverance. When the Israelites forget God, He allows them to be oppressed by a neighboring country. Then they cry out to God, and He raises up judges to deliver His people. The familiar story of the mighty Samson is found in this book.

RUTH

Writer: Unknown

Date: 1375–1050 B.C.

Literary Style: Narrative

The events of Ruth take place during some of the darkest days in the history of Israel. It is a time when the nation lapses again and again into the worship of false gods. In sharp contrast to this is the shining testimony of one Gentile woman from Moab who remains faithful to God.

1 SAMUEL

Writer: Samuel, Nathan, and Gad

Date: Unknown

Literary Style: Narrative

This book records a crucial time in Israel's history. Here the people of Israel reject God's chosen leader Samuel—a judge—and demand a king. Despite Samuel's warnings that a king will oppress them, the people insist that he anoint someone as king. So the leadership of Israel passes from Samuel to Saul, the nation's first king.

2 SAMUEL

Writer: Unknown

Date: 930 B.C.

Literary Style: Narrative

Second Samuel focuses on the life and career of Israel's greatest king—David. Under David, the kingdom of Israel doubles in size and its enemies are subdued. Though he is a good leader and popular with the people, David is not perfect. This book also records David's sin with Bathsheba and his tragic failure as a father.

1 KINGS

Writer: Unknown
Date: Unknown
Literary Style: Narrative

In 1 Kings, David's reign comes to an end and his son Solomon becomes king. God gives Solomon the gift of wisdom and the blessing of building the temple. By the end of his reign, the kingdom is in an agitated state of unrest due to the excessive taxes for all of his building projects. The book ends as Solomon's son Rehoboam takes the throne, which leads to the division of the kingdom.

2 KINGS

Writer: Unknown
Date: Unknown
Literary Style: Narrative

Second Kings shows the inability of God's people to rule themselves and the world. The kings of Israel and Judah turn their backs on God and lead their citizens astray. God sends many prophets to warn the people, but they refuse to listen. In the end, the kingdoms of Israel and Judah collapse, and their citizens are taken away into captivity.

1 CHRONICLES

Writer: Ezra
Date: 430 B.C.
Literary Style: Narrative

This book emphasizes the spiritual significance of David's righteous reign. Through David's offspring will come the Messiah, Jesus Christ, whose throne and kingdom will be established forever.

2 CHRONICLES

Writer: Ezra

Date: 430 B.C.

Literary Style: Narrative

The emphasis in 2 Chronicles is on the southern kingdom, Judah, and on David's descendants. Here God uses five outstanding kings to bring periods of revival, renewal, and reformation to the land.

EZRA

Writer: Ezra

Date: 450 B.C.

Literary Style: Narrative

Ezra relates the account of the two returns from Babylon. It picks up where 2 Chronicles leaves off by showing how God fulfills His promise to bring His people back after seventy years of exile and captivity.

NEHEMIAH

Writer: Nehemiah

Date: 445–432 B.C.

Literary Style: Narrative

The book of Nehemiah is a wonderful story of how to handle opposition and discouragement when you are seeking to serve the Lord. Nehemiah is a cupbearer for the king of Persia. After hearing about the danger the city of Jerusalem is in, he returns there and, despite local opposition, completes reconstruction of the walls and gates of the city in fifty-two days.

ESTHER

Writer: Unknown

Date: 483–471 B.C.

Literary Style: Narrative

The book of Esther shows God's providence at work in a profound way. As one Persian noble close to the king plots to kill the Jews, Esther, the Jewish queen, intercedes at great personal risk on behalf of her people.

JOB

Writer: Possibly Job

Date: Unknown

Literary Style: Poetry

The book of Job addresses one of life's most-asked questions: Why does God allow suffering? Despite the fact that Job loses everything, suffers greatly, and has doubts about God, he remains faithful to God. In the end, God blesses him greatly.

PSALMS

Writers: David, Asaph, the sons of Korah, Solomon, Heman, Ethan, and Moses

Date: 1440–586 B.C.

Literary Style: Poetry

The book of Psalms contains a variety of themes that touch on every area of life. The central theme, however, is the praise and worship of a sovereign and loving God. Besides being a source of comfort and worship, the Psalms are filled with prophecies about Jesus Christ.

PROVERBS

Writers: Solomon, Agur, and Lemuel

Date: Early in Solomon's reign

Literary Style: Wisdom Literature

Proverbs is a book of wisdom written by the wisest man who ever lived: Solomon. This book contains God's divine wisdom for every area of life, such as choosing friends, handling temptation, raising children, and knowing God.

ECCLESIASTES

Writer: Solomon

Date: 935 B.C.

Literary Style: Wisdom Literature

Ecclesiastes is Solomon's analysis of life. Solomon has everything—incredible wealth, power, and intellect. He tries every enterprise and every pleasure known to man. Yet his final conclusion about life is that it is empty and purposeless without God.

SONG OF SONGS

Writer: Solomon

Date: Unknown

Literary Style: Poetry

The Song of Songs is one of the most unusual books in the Bible. On one level, it is an expression of pure love—as God intended it—in marriage. On another level, it symbolically speaks of God's love for His people and their love for Him.

ISAIAH

Writer: Isaiah

Date: 700–681 B.C.

Literary Style: Prophecy

The book of Isaiah begins the prophetic portion of the Bible. It includes warnings of God's coming judgment upon the nations of Isaiah's day as well as prophecies about the future redeemer of humankind—Jesus Christ.

JEREMIAH

Writer: Jeremiah

Date: 627–586 B.C.

Literary Style: Prophecy

Jeremiah is known as the weeping prophet. He delivers God's messages to the people of Judah. Although he passionately pleads with them to repent of their sins and return to God, the people ignore him and are taken into captivity in Babylon.

LAMENTATIONS

Writer: Jeremiah

Date: 586 B.C.

Literary Style: Poetry and Prophecy

Lamentations is a book of sadness. It opens with Jeremiah weeping over the destruction of Jerusalem and the carting off of captives to Babylon. But near the end of the book, Jeremiah sees hope in the love and compassion of God.

EZEKIEL

Writer: Ezekiel
Date: 571 B.C.
Literary Style: Prophecy

Ezekiel is taken captive to Babylon twelve years before the fall of Jerusalem in 586 B.C. While there, he is called by God to preach to the captives a message of judgment and salvation, to call them to repentance and obedience. The book of Ezekiel also contains dramatic prophecy about the regathering of the nation Israel in the scheme of last days events.

DANIEL

Writer: Daniel
Date: 535 B.C.
Literary Style: Narrative and Prophecy

Like Ezekiel, Daniel is taken to Babylon in captivity, where he is trained to serve in the courts of the king. Through Daniel's writings, we learn of God's sovereignty and control of man's history. In addition, the book of Daniel contains some of the most well known stories in the Bible, including Daniel in the lions' den and the three men in the fiery furnace. It is also a powerful prophetic book and should be read to understand the book of Revelation.

HOSEA

Writer: Hosea
Date: 715 B.C.
Literary Style: Prophecy

Hosea is a tragic love story about God, who loves His people despite their unfaithfulness to Him. Hosea warns that one cannot disobey God without disastrous consequences. Yet this book dramatically portrays God's unending love and mercy as He offers forgiveness to those who repent.

JOEL

Writer: Joel
Date: 835–796 B.C.
Literary Style: Prophecy

This book describes God's inescapable and overwhelming judgment upon sinful people. The prophet Joel is sent to warn the people of the coming judgment of God. He calls for the people to turn back to God before judgment falls upon them.

AMOS

Writer: Amos
Date: 760–750 B.C.
Literary Style: Prophecy

Amos prophesies to the northern kingdom during a time of great prosperity. As a result of their prosperity, the people have become self-sufficient and indifferent toward God and others. Amos comes to warn them of the dangers of their indifference and spiritual complacency.

OBADIAH

Writer: Obadiah
Date: Possibly 627–586 B.C.
Literary Style: Prophecy

The book of Obadiah demonstrates God's ongoing protection of His people from their enemies. As the Babylonians carry the Israelites off in captivity, the Edomites watch in indifference. Therefore, Obadiah lets them know that they will stand condemned and be destroyed while Israel will be restored.

JONAH

Writer: Jonah

Date: 785–760 B.C.

Literary Style: Narrative

This is the story of a man who tries to run from God and quickly learns the futility of it. After repenting of his sin, Jonah is restored and recommissioned. His preaching results in a large revival as the entire city of Nineveh turns to God.

MICAH

Writer: Micah

Date: Possibly 742–687 B.C.

Literary Style: Prophecy

Micah gives us a glimpse of God's hatred of sin and, at the same time, his love for the sinner. This book also gives us some of the clearest predictions of the coming Messiah. Micah challenges us to live for God and join the faithful remnant of His people who live according to His will.

NAHUM

Writer: Nahum

Date: 663–654 B.C.

Literary Style: Prophecy

Nahum teaches that God is the righteous judge and the supreme ruler over all. Those who continually do evil and oppress God's people, ignoring His repeated warnings, will pay a price.

HABAKKUK

Writer: Habakkuk

Date: 612–589 B.C.

Literary Style: Prophecy

Habakkuk cannot understand how God can allow evil and injustice to persist in Judah. Yet as Habakkuk seeks God, he finds his answer in trusting God's character.

ZEPHANIAH

Writer: Zephaniah

Date: 640–621 B.C.

Literary Style: Prophecy

Zephaniah preaches during a time of religious revival in Judah. But the religious zeal is shallow and inconsistent. The people rid their homes—but not their hearts—of idols. Zephaniah warns them that God does not take sin lightly and that He will punish those who sin.

HAGGAI

Writer: Haggai

Date: 520 B.C.

Literary Style: Prophecy

After some of the Jews return from captivity, they begin to rebuild the destroyed temple. But due to opposition and spiritual apathy, they stop construction. Haggai calls the Jews to finish the temple. He encourages the people to wake up from their apathy and reorder their priorities, putting God first in their lives.

ZECHARIAH

Writer: Zechariah
Date: 520–480 B.C.
Literary Style: Prophecy

Zechariah ministers with Haggai during the rebuilding of the temple. He brings God's message of encouragement and hope to a discouraged people.

MALACHI

Writer: Malachi
Date: 430 B.C.
Literary Style: Prophecy

The book of Malachi is a beautiful expression of God's mercy and grace to a nation so unworthy of either. Israel, God's chosen people, willfully disobeys God. Yet like a father pleading with his children, God extends a hand of forgiveness to those who turn and faithfully follow after Him.

THE NEW TESTAMENT
MATTHEW

Writer: Matthew (Levi)
Date: 60–65 A.D.
Literary Style: Gospel

Matthew writes his Gospel with the Jew in mind and therefore includes many references to Old Testament prophecies that Jesus fulfills. It contains at least 129 quotations from or allusions to the Old Testament. Matthew's objective is to show the Jewish people that Jesus is indeed their long-awaited Messiah.

MARK

Writer: John Mark
Date: 55–65 A.D.
Literary Style: Gospel

The Gospel of Mark is the account of the life, ministry, miracles, and words of Jesus Christ. In contrast to Matthew, who primarily presents Jesus as the Messiah, Mark emphasizes the servanthood of the Lord.

LUKE

Writer: Luke
Date: 60 A.D.
Literary Style: Gospel

Luke is a Gentile who put his faith in Jesus Christ. His purpose for writing an account of Jesus Christ's life, death, and resurrection is to make the message of salvation understandable to those outside the Jewish faith and culture.

JOHN

Writer: John
Date: 85–90 A.D.
Literary Style: Gospel

While the emphasis in the other three Gospels centers around the events in the life of Jesus, John often focuses upon the meaning of those events. For instance, while all four Gospels record the miracle of the feeding of the five thousand, only John gives us Jesus' message on the "Bread of Life," which follows that miracle. John writes this Gospel so that people might believe, and he puts special emphasis on the deity of Jesus Christ.

ACTS

Writer: Luke
Date: 63–70 A.D.
Literary Style: History

This book shows the church's early development and rapid growth. It reveals how the dynamic power of the Holy Spirit transforms a diverse group of fishermen, tax collectors, and other ordinary folks into people who turn their world upside down with the gospel of Jesus Christ.

ROMANS

Writer: Paul
Date: 70 A.D.
Literary Style: Epistle (letter)

This letter to the church at Rome contains some of the prime secrets of the Christian life. It is a hard-hitting diagnosis of the primary source of people's problems—sin. It also shows the futility of thinking that the answers to our problems lie within ourselves. It is a foundational book that must be carefully studied by every Christian.

1 CORINTHIANS

Writer: Paul
Date: 55 A.D.
Literary Style: Epistle

Paul writes this epistle in response to certain situations that have arisen in the Corinthian church. He straightforwardly deals with many of the errors that the people of this church believe and practice. Among these pitfalls are sins of immorality, false teachings, and problems regarding marriage and lawsuits. This book contains foundational teaching on the proper use of the gifts of the Spirit.

2 CORINTHIANS

Writer: Paul

Date: 55–57 A.D.

Literary Style: Epistle

Some of the Corinthians still living in sin after Paul's first letter have begun to deny Paul's authority. Paul writes this second letter to deal with the problems that persist within the Corinthian church.

GALATIANS

Writer: Paul

Date: 49 A.D.

Literary Style: Epistle

Galatians is a foundational study that shows how complete the work of Jesus' death on the cross is for our salvation. Nothing needs to be added to that work—nor does it need to be improved upon—for you can't improve upon perfection.

EPHESIANS

Writer: Paul

Date: 60 A.D.

Literary Style: Epistle

The book of Ephesians shows us our rightful position as children of God "in the heavenlies" with Jesus Christ. It tells us of all that God has done for us, as well as how to fully appreciate and implement it practically in our lives. This book also contains essential teaching on spiritual warfare and the Christian family.

PHILIPPIANS

Writer: Paul
Date: 61 A.D.
Literary Style: Epistle

This book explains the mind-set, attitude, and outlook the believer must have if he or she is going to experience the joy of the Lord in a troubled world.

COLOSSIANS

Writer: Paul
Date: 60 A.D.
Literary Style: Epistle

Paul writes this epistle to refute certain false teachings that have found their way into the church at Colosse. A common theme of this book is the superiority of Jesus Christ.

1 THESSALONIANS

Writer: Paul
Date: 51 A.D.
Literary Style: Epistle

The theme of this letter focuses upon living a godly and holy life as we await the return of Jesus Christ. Paul also offers words of comfort concerning Christian loved ones who have died.

2 THESSALONIANS

Writer: Paul
Date: 51 A.D.
Literary Style: Epistle

This letter offers encouragement to believers who are facing persecution. It also offers correct teaching on the subject of "the day of the Lord," a confusing matter for some of the Thessalonian believers.

In addition, some Thessalonians are not living as they should in light of the return of the Lord, so Paul addresses that issue as well.

1 TIMOTHY

Writer: Paul

Date: 64 A.D.

Literary Style: Epistle

Paul, under the inspiration of the Holy Spirit, lays out what the conduct of the church and its leaders should be. Though Timothy himself is a pastor, these words apply to all who want to be used by God and have their lives make a difference.

2 TIMOTHY

Writer: Paul

Date: 67 A.D.

Literary Style: Epistle

Paul writes this second letter to Timothy to encourage him to be faithful to Christ. Paul also includes a glimpse of what the last days will look like. This is the final epistle that Paul writes before his death.

TITUS

Writer: Paul

Date: 65 A.D.

Literary Style: Epistle

Paul writes this letter to address the challenges facing Titus as an overseer of the churches on the island of Crete. He includes criteria for qualifications of leadership, sound teaching, and good works.

PHILEMON

Writer: Paul
Date: 60 A.D.
Literary Style: Epistle

This short but profound epistle contains a wonderful story of the importance of forgiveness among Christians.

HEBREWS

Writer: Unknown
Date: 68 A.D.
Literary Style: Epistle

The book of Hebrews is written for Jews who have accepted Jesus as their Messiah. It warns them of the danger of slipping back into the traditions of Judaism because they haven't put their roots down in the soil of Christianity.

JAMES

Writer: James, Jesus' half-brother
Date: 49 A.D.
Literary Style: Epistle

James speaks a lot about faith in his book, with an emphasis on results. He stresses the need to live a practical, seven-days-a-week, working faith.

1 PETER

Writer: Peter
Date: 65 A.D.
Literary Style: Epistle

The theme of Peter's first epistle is suffering. He brings inspired words of comfort to those who suffer under persecution.

2 PETER

Writer: Peter
Date: 66 A.D.
Literary Style: Epistle

In this epistle Peter reminds the believers of certain important spiritual truths. Peter also warns of false teachers and speaks of the hope of the coming of the Lord.

1 JOHN

Writer: John
Date: 90–95 A.D.
Literary Style: Epistle

In this letter John points out that a person either is or is not a child of God. There is no middle ground. John clearly emphasizes that if one is really a child of God, it is evident in one's outward behavior.

2 JOHN

Writer: John
Date: 90–95 A.D.
Literary Style: Epistle

In this letter John points out that true Christian love involves more than just an emotional feeling. It is grounded in what is true. John also warns of false teachers, urging believers not to receive them.

3 JOHN

Writer: John
Date: 90–95 A.D.
Literary Style: Epistle

John writes this letter to commend a believer named Gaius for the hospitality he shows to traveling teachers of the gospel.

JUDE

Writer: Jude, Jesus' half-brother
Date: 65 A.D.
Literary Style: Epistle

The book of Jude is one of the shortest books in the New Testament. Its theme centers around the great apostasy, or falling away from the faith, that will happen on earth before the return of Jesus Christ.

REVELATION

Writer: John
Date: 95 A.D.
Literary Style: Apocalyptic

In this great book we learn of the return of Jesus Christ to the earth, as well as the events preceding that climactic moment. Again, it is the only book of the Bible that promises a special blessing to the person who hears and keeps its truths.

52 GREAT BIBLE STORIES

The following list not only gives you the fifty-two Bible stories you should be familiar with as a Christian, it provides an interesting reading plan as well. Using the list below, you can read through one great Bible story a week for a whole year.

1. IN THE BEGINNING (GENESIS 1:1—2:4)
In an incredible display of majesty and power, God creates the heavens and the earth and everything in them.

2. THE FIRST SIN (GENESIS 2:5—3:24)
God's original plan for humankind is spoiled in one small but deliberate act of disobedience that enables sin to enter the human race.

3. NOAH AND THE ARK (GENESIS 6:1—9:17)

One man's faith in and obedience to God spares his family from certain death in the greatest flood ever experienced by humankind.

4. SODOM AND GOMORRAH (GENESIS 18:16—19:29)

Lot, a God-fearing man, allows outside influences and selfish pursuits to cloud his thinking. Though he escapes the destruction of his evil hometown, his compromising decisions leave a devastating mark on his life and family.

5. ABRAHAM AND ISAAC (GENESIS 22:1-18)

Abraham learns that complete obedience can mean great sacrifice—but also great blessing.

6. THE STORY OF JOSEPH (GENESIS 37:1-36; 39:1—45:28)

Despite his virtuous lifestyle and his love for God, nothing seems to go right for Joseph. Yet Joseph's personal faith empowers him to rise above his trials and temptations, and he ultimately finds strength and blessing in spite of his hardships.

7. THE BURNING BUSH (EXODUS 3:1—4:17)

While tending sheep in the desert, Moses sees an unusual sight that leads him into a personal encounter with the living God.

8. THE TEN PLAGUES (EXODUS 7:14—12:30)

Pharaoh refuses to let the Israelites leave Egypt. To convince Pharaoh to change his mind, God sends a series of plagues. Unfortunately, Pharaoh's pride ends up costing him something precious—the life of his firstborn son.

9. THE GREAT ESCAPE (EXODUS 12:31—14:31)

Moses and the Israelites overcome tremendous obstacles and learn the importance of completely trusting in God as they make their way to the Promised Land.

10. THE TWELVE SCOUTS AND THEIR REPORT (NUMBERS 13:1—14:45)

When Caleb and Joshua choose to follow God's orders despite popular opinion, they appear to be in trouble. God, however, turns the tables in their favor.

11. BALAAM AND THE TALKING DONKEY (NUMBERS 22:21-35)

Balaam tests God by going against His will—for profit. Fortunately, Balaam's donkey saves him from God's wrath.

12. THE BATTLE OF JERICHO (JOSHUA 5:13—6:27)

Marching and music play a strategic role in this unusual battle plan. Nevertheless, when the Israelites follow God's orders, they win a mighty victory. This story shows faith in action.

13. THE STORY OF GIDEON AND HIS ARMY (JUDGES 6:1—7:25)

Gideon feels completely unfit for God's service, yet he learns how much God can accomplish with very little.

14. THE RISE AND FALL OF SAMSON (JUDGES 13:1—16:31)

God wants to use Samson for His purposes, but Samson allows pride and lust to ruin his potential. He is a "he-man" with a "she-weakness." In spite of Samson's disobedience, God still extends grace to him in the end.

15. THE STORY OF RUTH (RUTH 1:1—4:22)

One of the greatest love stories ever! Ruth, young and widowed, chooses to leave her home for an unknown land and an uncertain future in order to care for her mother-in-law and worship the one true God. God blesses Ruth for her tender faith in a profound and special way.

16. THE CALLING OF SAMUEL (1 SAMUEL 1:1—3:21)

God uses the most unlikely person, a small child, to deliver a devastating message to Eli the priest.

17. DAVID AND GOLIATH (1 SAMUEL 17:1-58)

David overcomes seemingly insurmountable odds and silences his skeptics when he kills Goliath, the mighty Philistine warrior, with a few small stones and an unshakable faith in God.

18. TRUE FRIENDS (1 SAMUEL 20:1-42)

David and Jonathan overcome tremendous odds to become the best of friends.

19. DAVID SINS WITH BATHSHEBA (2 SAMUEL 11:1—12:25)

David underestimates his potential to fall when he allows lust to control his thoughts. He soon discovers that one act of passion can lead to a lifetime of regret.

20. ELIJAH AND THE PROPHETS OF BAAL (1 KINGS 18:16-40)

The prophet Elijah puts his faith on the line when he challenges the religious leaders of a pagan deity to match the mighty work of his God.

21. NAAMAN THE LEPER (2 KINGS 5:1-27)

A servant girl tells Naaman's wife about a prophet in Israel who can heal Naaman of his leprosy. With hope, the great commander Naaman looks for the prophet—Elisha—to heal him. But what Elisha tells Naaman to do requires faith.

22. LEPERS DISCOVER AN ABANDONED CAMP (2 KINGS 7:3-16)

In desperation, four starving lepers leave the safety of Samaria's gates to surrender to the enemy army that has besieged the city. Hoping to be fed, the lepers discover something even better.

23. HEZEKIAH'S ILLNESS (2 KINGS 20:1-11)

On his deathbed, Hezekiah, the king of Judah, prays to the Lord asking Him to remember his faithfulness and devotion. In an incredible act of mercy, God spares Hezekiah's life and even adds fifteen years to it.

24. JEHOSHAPHAT DEFEATS MOAB AND AMMON (2 CHRONICLES 20:1-30)

Jehoshaphat leans upon the Lord and His wisdom when faced with a great battle—and Jehoshaphat wins overwhelmingly.

25. NEHEMIAH REBUILDS THE WALL (NEHEMIAH 1:1-7:3)

One man's faith helps him persevere through adversity and accomplish a great task.

26. THE STORY OF QUEEN ESTHER (ESTHER 1:1—10:3)

Queen Esther has it all, yet she is willing to give up everything in order to obey God and save her people, the Jews.

27. THE STORY OF SHADRACH, MESHACH, AND ABEDNEGO (DANIEL 3:1-30)

These three men refuse to follow orders that contradict God's law. In the end, their uncompromising stance changes the heart of a selfish tyrant.

28. DANIEL IN THE LIONS' DEN (DANIEL 6:1-28)

Daniel takes his faith so seriously that he does not fear when it leads to persecution. He realizes that God is ultimately in control—even in a lions' den.

29. JONAH AND THE GREAT FISH (JONAH 1:1—4:11)

Jonah finds that it does not pay to run away from God and His plan for your life.

30. JESUS' BIRTH (MATTHEW 1:18-25; LUKE 1:26-38; 2:1-7)

This is the real Christmas story! In the most humble and amazing circumstances, the Savior of the world is born.

31. JESUS VISITS THE TEMPLE AS A BOY (LUKE 2:41-52)

As Jesus' parents return home from the Passover feast in Jerusalem, they notice that Jesus is not with them. Where they find Him and what they find Him doing astonishes them.

32. JESUS' BAPTISM (MATTHEW 3:13-17; MARK 1:9-11; LUKE 3:21-22)

At Jesus' baptism, God expresses His pleasure in His Son and calls Him to public ministry.

33. SATAN TEMPTS JESUS (MATTHEW 4:1-11; MARK 1:12-13; LUKE 4:1-13)

Jesus withstands temptation from the devil himself, giving His followers a model to follow when they encounter temptation.

34. JESUS CLEARS THE TEMPLE (MATTHEW 21:12-17; MARK 11:15-19; LUKE 19:45-48)

In one bold act, Jesus shows His zeal for God's house, making bitter enemies in the process.

35. JESUS AND THE MIRACULOUS CATCH OF FISH (LUKE 5:1-11)

Jesus' disciples reap great dividends when they follow Jesus' unusual advice.

36. JESUS AND THE SAMARITAN WOMAN (JOHN 4:1-30)

A woman who has spent her life looking for love finds true fulfillment and joy in Jesus Christ.

37. JESUS CALMS THE STORM AT SEA (MATTHEW 8:23-27; MARK 4:35-41; LUKE 8:22-25)

The disciples discover that although life can be unpredictable, Jesus can calm the storms.

38. JESUS HEALS A LAME MAN (JOHN 5:1-15)

A lame man who has been waiting for healing for more than thirty years receives immediate healing when he follows Jesus' instructions.

39. JESUS FEEDS FIVE THOUSAND (MATTHEW 14:13-21; MARK 6:30-44; LUKE 9:10-17; JOHN 6:1-14)

A little boy's lunch becomes the focal point of one of Jesus' greatest recorded miracles.

40. THE PARABLE OF THE GOOD SAMARITAN (LUKE 10:25-37)

The person we should consider to be our neighbor or friend may not be the person we expect, as this parable explains.

41. JESUS HEALS A BLIND MAN (JOHN 9:1-41)

This man not only receives his physical sight but also his spiritual sight as he sees Jesus for who He is.

42. JESUS RAISES LAZARUS FROM THE DEAD (JOHN 11:1-44)

While Lazarus's sisters expect Jesus to perform a healing, Jesus chooses to do something far greater.

43. THE PRODIGAL SON (LUKE 15:11-32)

Jesus illustrates God's mercy and forgiveness in this parable of a wayward son, and shows us how to get right with God.

44. ZACCHAEUS CLIMBS A SYCAMORE TREE (LUKE 19:1-10)

A lonely and despised man finds love and forgiveness in Jesus.

45. THE LAST SUPPER (MATTHEW 26:20-30; MARK 14:17-26; LUKE 22:14-30; JOHN 13:1-30)

Jesus uses some of His last moments with His disciples to teach them important lessons about servanthood and the meaning of His impending sacrifice.

46. JESUS' CRUCIFIXION (MATTHEW 27:15-66; MARK 15:2-47; LUKE 23:1-56; JOHN 18:28—19:42)

The Son of God shows His tremendous love for people by enduring the most humiliating torture and execution befitting the worst criminal.

47. JESUS' RESURRECTION (MATTHEW 28:1-10; MARK 16:1-8; LUKE 24:1-12; JOHN 20:1-18)

Christ's death seems to be a hopeless situation. But what His followers don't know is that He will rise from the dead and break sin's hold on humankind. This is truly the greatest true story of all.

48. PETER'S FIRST SERMON (ACTS 2:14-41)

A once dejected and disloyal follower, Peter shows his love for Jesus by preaching a powerful sermon through which many come to faith in Christ.

49. SAUL'S CONVERSION (ACTS 9:1-19)

One of the earliest persecutors of Christians becomes a believer while he is on his way to arrest Christians in Damascus.

50. AN ANGEL RESCUES PETER FROM PRISON (ACTS 12:1-19)

A prayer meeting receives a dramatic answer in the middle of the night.

51. PAUL AND SILAS IN PRISON (ACTS 16:16-40)

Paul and Silas rise above their circumstances by praising God for His goodness through their trials.

52. PAUL'S JOURNEY TO ROME (ACTS 27:1—28:16)

A seemingly hopeless situation turns into a tremendous witnessing opportunity for the apostle Paul.

THROUGH THE NEW TESTAMENT IN A YEAR

JANUARY

FEBRUARY

01 Matthew 13:24-35; Romans 11:7-12
02 Matthew 13:36-43; Romans 11:13-21
03 Matthew 13:44-58; Romans 11:22-27
04 Matthew 14:1-12; Romans 11:28-36
05 Matthew 14:13-21; Romans 12:1-5
06 Matthew 14:22-36; Romans 12:6-13
07 Matthew 15:1-20; Romans 12:14-21
08 Matthew 15:21-28; Romans 13:1-7
09 Matthew 15:29-39; Romans 13:8-14
10 Matthew 16:1-12; Romans 14:1-4
11 Matthew 16:13-28; Romans 14:5-9
12 Matthew 17:1-13; Romans 14:10-16
13 Matthew 17:14-21; Romans 14:17-23
14 Matthew 17:22-27; Romans 15:1-6
15 Matthew 18:1-20; Romans 15:7-17
16 Matthew 18:21-35; Romans 15:18-22
17 Matthew 19:1-12; Romans 15:23-33
18 Matthew 19:13-15; Romans 16:1-16
19 Matthew 19:16-30; Romans 16:17-27
20 Matthew 20:1-19; 1 Corinthians 1:1-9
21 Matthew 20:20-28; 1 Corinthians 1:10-17
22 Matthew 20:29-34; 1 Corinthians 1:18-25
23 Matthew 21:1-17; 1 Corinthians 1:26-31
24 Matthew 21:18-22; 1 Corinthians 2:1-10
25 Matthew 21:23-46; 1 Corinthians 2:11-16
26 Matthew 22:1-14; 1 Corinthians 3:1-9
27 Matthew 22:15-46; 1 Corinthians 3:10-17
28 Matthew 23:1-12;1 Corinthians 3:18-23

MARCH

01 Matthew 23:13-39; 1 Corinthians 4:1-7
02 Matthew 24:1-31; 1 Corinthians 4:8-13
03 Matthew 24:32-51; 1 Corinthians 4:14-21
04 Matthew 25:1-13; 1 Corinthians 5:1-8
05 Matthew 25:14-30; 1 Corinthians 5:9-13
06 Matthew 25:31-46; 1 Corinthians 6:1-8
07 Matthew 26:1-16; 1 Corinthians 6:9-13
08 Matthew 26:17-35; 1 Corinthians 6:14-20

09 Matthew 26:36-56; 1 Corinthians 7:1-9
10 Matthew 26:57-75; 1 Corinthians 7:10-17
11 Matthew 27:1-10; 1 Corinthians 7:18-24
12 Matthew 27:11-30; 1 Corinthians 7:25-31
13 Matthew 27:31-56; 1 Corinthians 7:32-40
14 Matthew 27:57-66; 1 Corinthians 8:1-13
15 Matthew 28:1-15; 1 Corinthians 9:1-10
16 Matthew 28:16-20; 1 Corinthians 9:11-18
17 Mark 1:1-8; 1 Corinthians 9:19-27
18 Mark 1:9-13; 1 Corinthians 10:1-14
19 Mark 1:14-20; 1 Corinthians 10:15-22
20 Mark 1:21-28; 1 Corinthians 10:23–11:1
21 Mark 1:29-39; 1 Corinthians 11:2-16
22 Mark 1:40-45; 1 Corinthians 11:17-22
23 Mark 2:1-12; 1 Corinthians 11:23-34
24 Mark 2:13-17; 1 Corinthians 12:1-3
25 Mark 2:18-22; 1 Corinthians 12:4-11
26 Mark 2:23–3:6; 1 Corinthians 12:12-18
27 Mark 3:7-19; 1 Corinthians 12:19-27
28 Mark 3:20-35; 1 Corinthians 12:28-31
29 Mark 4:1-20; 1 Corinthians 13:1-7
30 Mark 4:21-34; 1 Corinthians 13:8-13
31 Mark 4:35-41; 1 Corinthians 14:1-5

APRIL

01 Mark 5:1-20; 1 Corinthians 14:6-12
02 Mark 5:21-43; 1 Corinthians 14:13-17
03 Mark 6:1-6; 1 Corinthians 14:18-25
04 Mark 6:7-13; 1 Corinthians 14:26-32
05 Mark 6:14-29; 1 Corinthians 14:33-40
06 Mark 6:30-44; 1 Corinthians 15:1-11
07 Mark 6:45-56; 1 Corinthians 15:12-20
08 Mark 7:1-23; 1 Corinthians 15:21-28
09 Mark 7:24-37; 1 Corinthians 15:29-34
10 Mark 8:1-10; 1 Corinthians 15:35-44
11 Mark 8:11-21; 1 Corinthians 15:45-49
12 Mark 8:22-26; 1 Corinthians 15:50-58
13 Mark 8:27-38; 1 Corinthians 16:1-9
14 Mark 9:1-13; 1 Corinthians 16:10-18
15 Mark 9:14-29; 1 Corinthians 16:19-24

16 Mark 9:30-37; 2 Corinthians 1:1-7
17 Mark 9:38-50; 2 Corinthians 1:8-14
18 Mark 10:1-12; 2 Corinthians 1:15-24
19 Mark 10:13-16; 2 Corinthians 2:1-4
20 Mark 10:17-31; 2 Corinthians 2:5-11
21 Mark 10:32-45; 2 Corinthians 2:12-17
22 Mark 10:46-52; 2 Corinthians 3:1-6
23 Mark 11:1-11; 2 Corinthians 3:7-18
24 Mark 11:12-27; 2 Corinthians 4:1-7
25 Mark 11:28–12:12; 2 Corinthians 4:8-17
26 Mark 12:13-34; 2 Corinthians 4:18–5:10
27 Mark 12:35-44; 2 Corinthians 5:11-21
28 Mark 13:1-13; 2 Corinthians 6:1-7
29 Mark 13:14-37; 2 Corinthians 6:8-13
30 Mark 14:1-11; 2 Corinthians 6:14–7:4

MAY

01 Mark 14:12-31; 2 Corinthians 7:5-10
02 Mark 14:32-52; 2 Corinthians 7:11-16
03 Mark 14:53-72; 2 Corinthians 8:1-8
04 Mark 15:1-20; 2 Corinthians 8:9-15
05 Mark 15:21-32; 2 Corinthians 8:16-24
06 Mark 15:33-47; 2 Corinthians 9:1-5
07 Mark 16:1-20; 2 Corinthians 9:6-15
08 Luke 1:1-25; 2 Corinthians 10:1-6
09 Luke 1:26-56; 2 Corinthians 10:7-12
10 Luke 1:57-80; 2 Corinthians 10:13-18
11 Luke 2:1-20; 2 Corinthians 11:1-6
12 Luke 2:21-40; 2 Corinthians 11:7-15
13 Luke 2:41-52; 2 Corinthians 11:16-33
14 Luke 3:1-18; 2 Corinthians 12:1-10
15 Luke 3:19-23a; 2 Corinthians 12:11-15
16 Luke 3:23b-38; 2 Corinthians 12:16-21
17 Luke 4:1-13; 2 Corinthians 13:1-6
18 Luke 4:14-30; 2 Corinthians 13:7-14
19 Luke 4:31-44; Galatians 1:1-5
20 Luke 5:1-11; Galatians 1:6-12
21 Luke 5:12-16; Galatians 1:13-24
22 Luke 5:17-26; Galatians 2:1-5
23 Luke 5:27-39; Galatians 2:6-10

24 Luke 6:1-11; Galatians 2:11-16
25 Luke 6:12-16; Galatians 2:17-21
26 Luke 6:17-38; Galatians 3:1-9
27 Luke 6:39-49; Galatians 3:10-14
28 Luke 7:1-10; Galatians 3:15-20
29 Luke 7:11-17; Galatians 3:21-29
30 Luke 7:18-35; Galatians 4:1-7
31 Luke 7:36-50; Galatians 4:8-11

JUNE

01 Luke 8:1-3; Galatians 4:12-20
02 Luke 8:4-15; Galatians 4:21-31
03 Luke 8:16-18; Galatians 5:1-6
04 Luke 8:19-21; Galatians 5:7-15
05 Luke 8:22-25; Galatians 5:16-21
06 Luke 8:26-40; Galatians 5:22-26
07 Luke 8:41-56; Galatians 6:1-10
08 Luke 9:1-9; Galatians 6:11-18
09 Luke 9:10-17; Ephesians 1:1-8
10 Luke 9:18-22; Ephesians 1:9-14
11 Luke 9:23-27; Ephesians 1:15-23
12 Luke 9:28-36; Ephesians 2:1-7
13 Luke 9:37-43a; Ephesians 2:8-13
14 Luke 9:43b-50; Ephesians 2:14-22
15 Luke 9:51-62; Ephesians 3:1-7
16 Luke 10:1-24; Ephesians 3:8-13
17 Luke 10:25-37; Ephesians 3:14-21
18 Luke 10:38-42; Ephesians 4:1-10
19 Luke 11:1-13; Ephesians 4:11-16
20 Luke 11:14-28; Ephesians 4:17-24
21 Luke 11:29-36; Ephesians 4:25-32
22 Luke 11:37-54; Ephesians 5:1-9
23 Luke 12:1-12; Ephesians 5:10-20
24 Luke 12:13-34; Ephesians 5:21-33
25 Luke 12:35-48; Ephesians 6:1-4
26 Luke 12:49-59; Ephesians 6:5-9
27 Luke 13:1-9; Ephesians 6:10-17
28 Luke 13:10-17; Ephesians 6:18-24
29 Luke 13:18-21; Philippians 1:1-6
30 Luke 13:22-30; Philippians 1:7-11

JULY

01 Luke 13:31-35; Philippians 1:12-18a
02 Luke 14:1-6; Philippians 1:18b-30
03 Luke 14:7-24; Philippians 2:1-11
04 Luke 14:25-35; Philippians 2:12-18
05 Luke 15:1-10; Philippians 2:19-30
06 Luke 15:11-32; Philippians 3:1-7
07 Luke 16:1-14; Philippians 3:8-12
08 Luke 16:15-31; Philippians 3:13-16
09 Luke 17:1-4; Philippians 3:17-21
10 Luke 17:5-10; Philippians 4:1-7
11 Luke 17:11-19; Philippians 4:8-14
12 Luke 17:20-37; Philippians 4:15-23
13 Luke 18:1-8; Colossians 1:1-6
14 Luke 18:9-17; Colossians 1:7-9
15 Luke 18:18-30; Colossians 1:10-14
16 Luke 18:31-34; Colossians 1:15-18
17 Luke 18:35-43; Colossians 1:19-23
18 Luke 19:1-10; Colossians 1:24-29
19 Luke 19:11-27; Colossians 2:1-10
20 Luke 19:28-40; Colossians 2:11-15
21 Luke 19:41-48; Colossians 2:16-23
22 Luke 20:1-19; Colossians 3:1-8
23 Luke 20:20-26; Colossians 3:9-14
24 Luke 20:27-47; Colossians 3:15-17
25 Luke 21:1-4; Colossians 3:18–4:1
26 Luke 21:5-19; Colossians 4:2-6
27 Luke 21:20-38; Colossians 4:7-18
28 Luke 22:1-23; 1 Thessalonians 1:1-10
29 Luke 22:24-30; 1 Thessalonians 2:1-8
30 Luke 22:31-34; 1 Thessalonians 2:9-13
31 Luke 22:35-38; 1 Thessalonians 2:14–3:4

AUGUST

01 Luke 22:39-53; 1 Thessalonians 3:5-8
02 Luke 22:54-62; 1 Thessalonians 3:9-13
03 Luke 22:63-71; 1 Thessalonians 4:1-8
04 Luke 23:1-25; 1 Thessalonians 4:9-12
05 Luke 23:26-43; 1 Thessalonians 4:13–5:3

06 Luke 23:44-56; 1 Thessalonians 5:4-11
07 Luke 24:1-12; 1 Thessalonians 5:12-22
08 Luke 24:13-34; 1 Thessalonians 5:23-28
09 Luke 24:35-53; 2 Thessalonians 1:1-12
10 John 1:1-14; 2 Thessalonians 2:1-6
11 John 1:15-34; 2 Thessalonians 2:7-17
12 John 1:35-51; 2 Thessalonians 3:1-5
13 John 2:1-12; 2 Thessalonians 3:6-18
14 John 2:13-25; 1 Timothy 1:1-6
15 John 3:1-21; 1 Timothy 1:7-11
16 John 3:22-36; 1 Timothy 1:12-17
17 John 4:1-30; 1 Timothy 1:18-20
18 John 4:31-42; 1 Timothy 2:1-8
19 John 4:43-54; 1 Timothy 2:9-15
20 John 5:1-24; 1 Timothy 3:1-7
21 John 5:25-47; 1 Timothy 3:8-15
22 John 6:1-15; 1 Timothy 3:16–4:6
23 John 6:16-21; 1 Timothy 4:7-11
24 John 6:22-46; 1 Timothy 4:12–5:2
25 John 6:47-71; 1 Timothy 5:3-10
26 John 7:1-13; 1 Timothy 5:11-16
27 John 7:14-36; 1 Timothy 5:17-25
28 John 7:37-53; 1 Timothy 6:1-5
29 John 8:1-11; 1 Timothy 6:6-12
30 John 8:12-30; 1 Timothy 6:13-16
31 John 8:31-59; 1 Timothy 6:17-21

SEPTEMBER

01 John 9:1-12; 2 Timothy 1:1-7
02 John 9:13-41; 2 Timothy 1:8-14
03 John 10:1-21; 2 Timothy 1:15-18
04 John 10:22-42; 2 Timothy 2:1-7
05 John 11:1-29; 2 Timothy 2:8-14
06 John 11:30-46; 2 Timothy 2:15-21
07 John 11:47-57; 2 Timothy 2:22-26
08 John 12:1-11; 2 Timothy 3:1-9
09 John 12:12-19; 2 Timothy 3:10-17
10 John 12:20-36; 2 Timothy 4:1-4
11 John 12:37-50; 2 Timothy 4:5-8
12 John 13:1-20; 2 Timothy 4:9-22

13 John 13:21-38; Titus 1:1-5

14 John 14:1-14; Titus 1:6-16

15 John 14:15-31; Titus 2:1-10

16 John 15:1-15; Titus 2:11-15

17 John 15:16-27; Titus 3:1-8

18 John 16:1-15; Titus 3:9-15

19 John 16:16-33; Philemon 1:1-7

20 John 17:1-26; Philemon 1:8-25

21 John 18:1-14; Hebrews 1:1-14

22 John 18:15-27; Hebrews 2:1-4

23 John 18:28-40; Hebrews 2:5-10

24 John 19:1-15; Hebrews 2:11-15

25 John 19:16-30; Hebrews 2:16–3:6

26 John 19:31-42; Hebrews 3:7-14

27 John 20:1-18; Hebrews 3:15-19

28 John 20:19-31; Hebrews 4:1-6

29 John 21:1-14; Hebrews 4:7-13

30 John 21:15-25; Hebrews 4:14–5:6

OCTOBER

01 Acts 1:1-13; Hebrews 5:7-10

02 Acts 1:14-26; Hebrews 5:11-14

03 Acts 2:1-13; Hebrews 6:1-6

04 Acts 2:14-39; Hebrews 6:7-15

05 Acts 2:40-47; Hebrews 6:16-20

06 Acts 3:1-26; Hebrews 7:1-11

07 Acts 4:1-22; Hebrews 7:12-22

08 Acts 4:23-37; Hebrews 7:23-28

09 Acts 5:1-11; Hebrews 8:1-6

10 Acts 5:12-25; Hebrews 8:7-13

11 Acts 5:26-42; Hebrews 9:1-10

12 Acts 6:1-7; Hebrews 9:11-15

13 Acts 6:8–7:16; Hebrews 9:16-23

14 Acts 7:17-43; Hebrews 9:24-28

15 Acts 7:44-60; Hebrews 10:1-10

16 Acts 8:1-25; Hebrews 10:11-22

17 Acts 8:26-40; Hebrews 10:23-25

18 Acts 9:1-19a; Hebrews 10:26-31

19 Acts 9:19b-31; Hebrews 10:32-39

20 Acts 9:32-35; Hebrews 11:1-6

21 Acts 9:36-43; Hebrews 11:7-12

22 Acts 10:1-23a; Hebrews 11:13-16

23 Acts 10:23b-48; Hebrews 11:17-20

24 Acts 11:1-18; Hebrews 11:21-23

25 Acts 11:19-30; Hebrews 11:24-29

26 Acts 12:1-25; Hebrews 11:30-40

27 Acts 13:1-12; Hebrews 12:1-4

28 Acts 13:13-23; Hebrews 12:5-11

29 Acts 13:24-44; Hebrews 12:12-17

30 Acts 13:45-52; Hebrews 12:18-24

31 Acts 14:1-7; Hebrews 12:25-29

NOVEMBER

01 Acts 14:8-20a; Hebrews 13:1-9

02 Acts 14:20b-28; Hebrews 13:10-16

03 Acts 15:1-21; Hebrews 13:17-25

04 Acts 15:22-41; James 1:1-4

05 Acts 16:1-10; James 1:5-8

06 Acts 16:11-15; James 1:9-18

07 Acts 16:16-40; James 1:19-27

08 Acts 17:1-15; James 2:1-9

09 Acts 17:16-34; James 2:10-13

10 Acts 18:1-8; James 2:14-26

11 Acts 18:9-23; James 3:1-12

12 Acts 18:24-28; James 3:13-18

13 Acts 19:1-10; James 4:1-6

14 Acts 19:11-20; James 4:7-10

15 Acts 19:21-41; James 4:11-12

16 Acts 20:1-12; James 4:13-17

17 Acts 20:13-38; James 5:1-6

18 Acts 21:1-17; James 5:7-12

19 Acts 21:18-36; James 5:13-20

20 Acts 21:37–22:16; 1 Peter 1:1-7

21 Acts 22:17-29; 1 Peter 1:8-13

22 Acts 22:30–23:11; 1 Peter 1:14-25

23 Acts 23:12-35; 1 Peter 2:1-10

24 Acts 24:1-9; 1 Peter 2:11-16

25 Acts 24:10-27; 1 Peter 2:17-25

26 Acts 25:1-12; 1 Peter 3:1-6

27 Acts 25:13-27; 1 Peter 3:7-9

28 Acts 26:1-32; 1 Peter 3:10-16
29 Acts 27:1-15; 1 Peter 3:17-22
30 Acts 27:16-44; 1 Peter 4:1-6

DECEMBER

01 Acts 28:1-10; 1 Peter 4:7-11
02 Acts 28:11-31; 1 Peter 4:12-19
03 Revelation 1:1-8; 1 Peter 5:1-7
04 Revelation 1:9-20; 1 Peter 5:8-14
05 Revelation 2:1-7; 2 Peter 1:1-11
06 Revelation 2:8-11; 2 Peter 1:12-18
07 Revelation 2:12-17; 2 Peter 1:19–2:11
08 Revelation 2:18-29; 2 Peter 2:12-22
09 Revelation 3:1-6; 2 Peter 3:1-7
10 Revelation 3:7-13; 2 Peter 3:8-13
11 Revelation 3:14-22; 2 Peter 3:14-18
12 Revelation 4:1-11; 1 John 1:1-4
13 Revelation 5:1-14; 1 John 1:5-10
14 Revelation 6:1-17; 1 John 2:1-6
15 Revelation 7:1-17; 1 John 2:7-11
16 Revelation 8:1-13; 1 John 2:12-17
17 Revelation 9:1-21; 1 John 2:18-27
18 Revelation 10:1-11; 1 John 2:28–3:6
19 Revelation 11:1-19; 1 John 3:7-11
20 Revelation 12:1–13:1a; 1 John 3:12-24
21 Revelation 13:1b-18; 1 John 4:1-6
22 Revelation 14:1-7; 1 John 4:7-15
23 Revelation 14:8-20; 1 John 4:16-21
24 Revelation 15:1-8; 1 John 5:1-15
25 Revelation 16:1-21; 1 John 5:16-21
26 Revelation 17:1-18; 2 John 1:1-6
27 Revelation 18:1-24; 2 John 1:7-13
28 Revelation 19:1-21; 3 John 1:1-15
29 Revelation 20:1-15; Jude 1:1-7
30 Revelation 21:1–22:6; Jude 1:8-16
31 Revelation 22:7-21; Jude 1:17-25

PART TWO
PRAYER

SIX

THE POWER OF PRAYER

Have you ever been in an impossible situation, with no way out? Have you ever desperately wanted something but knew there was no way you could ever have it? Have you ever thought there's no future for you—that you're hopeless and it's too late to change?

If you've had such thoughts and feelings, you're not alone. Many people feel trapped by life's circumstances, unable to cope, thinking they can't go on. They need someone they can talk to, someone they can count on, someone to give them hope.

As a new believer in Jesus Christ, you've found the One who can give you that hope. You are in the process of learning that nothing is impossible with God; God can fulfill your needs (and sometimes even your dreams); you do have a future and a hope—it's never too late.

You are also learning that you can call on the Lord 24/7—which is to say, all day every day, from any place, for any reason. The way you do that is through prayer.

By prayer we come into God's presence. By prayer we talk to Him—about anything and everything. Just as you can talk over anything with a good friend, so you can call on God under any circumstances, for any reason.

Let's look at some examples from the Bible of people who knew when to pray. Each of them experienced the power of prayer firsthand. From their stories you will observe that prayer can dramatically change situations, people, and sometimes even the course of nature.

WHEN THINGS LOOK IMPOSSIBLE

Did you ever face something that felt just too big to handle? Did it seem like the odds were stacked against you and there was no way out? Take a chapter from the life of Old Testament king Jehoshaphat, who was doing the best he could when, without warning, the bottom dropped out of his life (see 2 Chronicles 19–20).

Jehoshaphat was one of the few good kings to reign over the southern kingdom of Judah. Despite a few slipups, he tried to follow the Lord and bring his nation back to the worship of God by destroying the idols that had been built in his land. Then one day he received word that a "vast army" of Moabites, Ammonites, and Meunites—much larger than the army he commanded—was marching against Judah. The odds were definitely against him.

The Bible tells us that Jehoshaphat was "alarmed." I should think so! But the first thing he did was turn to the Lord for guidance. Instead of worrying, he did just as the apostle Paul, centuries later, would instruct the church at Philippi: "Don't worry about anything; instead, pray about everything. Tell God what you need, and thank him for all he has done" (Philippians 4:6). Jehoshaphat took his "alarm" to God and sought His guidance.

Read the king's prayer in 2 Chronicles 20:5-12. In so many words he said, "Okay, God, You gave this land to us as a promise to Abraham. Then when our ancestors came here, You told us not to destroy the Moabites and Ammonites and the people of Mount Seir. In fact, if You remember, You told us not to even travel through their lands but to go the long way around! So we did as You said and left those people alone, and now they are the ones coming to attack us!"

Of course, God already knew all this, but Jehoshaphat laid out the situation before Him. Listen to Jehoshaphat's request: "O our God, won't you stop them? We are powerless against this mighty army that is about to attack us. We don't know what to do, but we are looking to you for help" (v. 12, NLT).

And God did indeed help.

Responding powerfully to the prayer of the king and his people, the Lord answered in dramatic fashion. Just read what happened in verses 13-30!

When you have an "impossible" need, remember that "nothing is impossible with God" (Luke 1:37). Talk to Him about it. He may not answer all your questions. He may not answer as quickly as He answered Jehoshaphat. Then again, He might! But you will have taken your need to the only One who can truly help, the almighty Creator of the universe. What more could you need?

WHEN YOU HAVE A DESIRE

Did you ever desire something very much? Sometimes the things we desire aren't good for us, and God knows it, so He says no to a request. Sometimes the things we desire are good, but not good at that particular time, so He tells us to wait. At other times He sees our pure hearts and motivations and answers with a resounding "yes," as He did with Hannah (see 1 Samuel 1).

Hannah was an Israelite who was unable to have children. Infertility is difficult and painful enough for women today, but in Hannah's day, it was considered a curse. To make matters worse, Hannah's husband had another wife who was able to have children, and she made fun of Hannah's infertility. Hannah's husband loved her very much, but she still wanted to a child.

Hannah took her request to God. You can read her prayer in 1 Samuel 1:11 (NLT): "O Lord Almighty, if you will look down upon my sorrow and answer my prayer and give me a son, then I will give him back to you. He will be yours for his entire lifetime, and as a sign that he has been dedicated to the Lord, his hair will never be cut."

God answered Hannah's prayer, and her child, Samuel, grew up to be a prophet who helped to heal the nation of Israel after the chaotic years under the judges.

Jesus promises that when our requests are in line with God's will, He will hear and answer. "You can ask for anything in my name, and I will do it, because the work of the Son brings glory to the Father. Yes, ask anything in my name, and I will do it!" (John 14:13-14, NLT).

Now, this doesn't necessarily mean you can ask for whatever you want and God will give it to you. The key is to discover the will of God and pray accordingly. Your requests will more likely be in line with His will when you are in tune with Him—learning about Him and what He wants you to do, obeying Him, and following Him. Then you can bring any and every request to God, trusting Him to do His will.

WHEN IT SEEMS TOO LATE

Can you pray even after you've messed things up?

Of course—otherwise God couldn't have listened to that first prayer you prayed in order to be saved. Sometimes we fail, but God is always ready to hear, forgive, and set us back on the right path to serve Him. If you find that hard to believe, take a look at the story of Samson (see Judges 13–16).

Samson had great potential. Like Hannah, Samson's mother had been unable to have children, but then an angel promised her a son (Judges 13:5). Her child would be very great and would "rescue Israel from the Philistines." Samson would be set aside for this special task and be a Nazirite—meaning he would have to keep certain vows during his lifetime, including never cutting his hair.

God did indeed use Samson's mighty strength to harass the Philistines, but sadly, Samson didn't stay close to the Lord. He got involved with a Philistine woman named Delilah and told her the secret of his great strength: "'My hair has never been cut,' he confessed, 'for I was dedicated to God as a Nazirite from birth. If my head were shaved, my strength would leave me, and I would become as weak as anyone else'" (Judges 16:17, NLT).

Delilah told Samson's secret to the Philistine leaders who had been desperately trying to find a way to stop his constant harassment. Delilah lulled Samson to sleep, cut his hair, and called in his enemies, who put him in chains, blinded him, and put him in prison.

But even after Samson's failure, God gave him another chance. The Philistines held a great celebration to thank their god for delivering Samson to them. They brought him out for entertainment, chaining him between two big pillars in their temple. Samson prayed, "Sovereign Lord, remember me again. O God, please strengthen me one more time so that I may pay back the Philistines for the loss of my eyes" (Judges 16:28).

And God answered his prayer. He gave Samson the strength to push over the pillars he was chained to and literally bring down the house! In the end, Samson played a part in God's plan to deliver his nation from the Philistines.

Satan knows that prayer is your lifeline to God. When you have sinned, Satan whispers in your ear, "Do you think God hears the prayers of someone like you? You're such a failure and hypocrite. Don't even think about praying!"

It's easy to fall for a ploy like that. But the truth is that when you have sinned, that is the time to pray! Your first prayer should be one of repentance, in which you acknowledge your wrongdoing and turn from it. Then, like Samson, you should ask God for another chance. He will graciously give it to you.

WHEN YOU DON'T UNDERSTAND

We don't understand all that happens in our lives. We don't see the "big picture" that God sees, so there are plenty of things we wonder about. But take your questions to God and place them in His capable hands. He wants you to trust Him even when you don't understand.

Paul and Silas were taking the gospel message to people who had never heard it. God had sent them a vision to go into an area called Macedonia.

The first place they visited was the city of Philippi. And what happened? They ended up stripped, beaten, flogged, and thrown into prison. They were put into the inner dungeon with their feet in stocks.

Now wait a minute! Weren't they doing just what God had called them to do? Yes, they were. And they were right where God wanted them at the moment. Content in that knowledge, what were Paul and Silas doing in that dark prison cell? Praying and singing hymns to God! (See Acts 16:25.)

The Bible doesn't tell us the words of their prayers, but we can guess that they weren't despairing cries of fear—not when they were also singing! Paul and Silas trusted God to do what He desired with them, for they were in His hands. They didn't understand, but they prayed.

A similar situation had occurred with the apostle Peter a few years earlier. He too had been imprisoned for teaching the gospel—doing just what God had called him to do. His fellow apostle James had just been killed by Herod for the same reason, and now Peter was on death row. And do you know what he was doing in prison? The Bible tells us he was sleeping! Not sitting awake wringing his hands, worried, scared—he was deep into dreamland.

But I imagine that he had done plenty of praying first, and the Bible tells us that other people were praying "very earnestly" for him as well. The church didn't understand God's ways; in fact, they may have questioned them. But they didn't stop praying. And Peter was miraculously set free! (Read his story in Acts 12:1-17.)

WHEN YOU FEEL ALONE

You may never be imprisoned for your faith, but that doesn't mean you don't have problems. Do you ever feel all alone—just you against the world? No one to turn to? No one who understands? Do you ever feel a sort of darkness overwhelm you with fear and depression?

Elijah is a Bible hero who understands those feelings.

A powerful prophet of God, Elijah was used in mighty ways to speak God's words to the string of evil kings that ruled the northern kingdom of Israel. He made himself plenty of enemies along the way, because he always brought bad news. (That's because the people were sinning against God—but they never made the connection!)

Perhaps Elijah is most famous for his contest with the prophets of the false god Baal on Mount Carmel. Jezebel, the queen of Israel, employed hundreds of false prophets, and Elijah invited them to a contest:

> "Now bring all the people of Israel to Mount Carmel, with all 450 prophets of Baal and the 400 prophets of Asherah, who are supported by Jezebel" (1 Kings 18:19).

Imagine that! Setting up a contest where the odds are 850 to 1 against you! But Elijah knew that the contest wasn't really between him and those prophets but between God and a powerless idol. Obviously, this was no contest at all. Elijah prayed to God to send down fire from heaven to show the people of Israel who was really God—and God answered.

Then Elijah prayed that God would end a seven-year drought by bringing rain—and God answered. But then Queen Jezebel put a price on Elijah's head, and he ran for his life. "He went on alone into the desert, traveling all day. He sat down under a solitary broom tree and prayed that he might die. 'I have had enough, Lord,' he said. 'Take my life, for I am no better than my ancestors'" (1 Kings 19:4).

His biggest complaint was that he thought he was the only worshiper of God left in the entire kingdom. Elijah told God his true feelings. God listened, let Elijah rest a bit, fed him, told him the truth, and then sent him back to work.

We can pray to God even when we feel the worst. In fact, He is the best One for us to go to. He understands, He answers, and He gets us going again.

GREAT POWER, WONDERFUL RESULTS

Some people ask, "Do I have to pray in a certain position to know I'll be answered?" Three ministers were debating this question. One minister shared that he felt the key was in the hands. He always held his hands together and pointed them upward as a symbolic form of worship.

Another minister suggested that real prayer was conducted on your knees. That was the only way to really pray.

The third said that they were both wrong. The only position in which to pray was to lie on the floor flat on your face.

As they were talking, a telephone repairman had been working in the background, overhearing their conversation. Finally, he could take it no longer. He blurted, "I found that the most powerful prayer I ever prayed was while I was dangling upside down by my heels from a power pole suspended forty feet above the ground!"

As we saw from the biblical examples in this chapter, we can pray in any position, anytime, anywhere. And remember Jonah, who prayed from the belly of a fish (see Jonah 2:1). God will hear your prayer wherever you are.

Without any mention of when, where, or how, the apostle James says to his readers, "The earnest prayer of a righteous person has great power and wonderful results" (James 5:16). As believers we are considered "righteous persons" even though we know we're not perfect yet. God sees us as "righteous" because He has forgiven us. So our prayers have great power and wonderful results.

We can communicate with God about any situation, at any time, in any way. He promises to hear and answer. He's just waiting to hear from you.

Do you have anything you need to pray about right now? A problem at work or school or with family or friends? Perhaps you need a healing touch from God. Maybe you need His wisdom for a certain situation.

Talk to your loving heavenly Father about it.

He's only a prayer away!

SEVEN
LORD, TEACH ME TO PRAY

The disciples observed Jesus' habit of going away to pray (sometimes all night). At one point, when He returned to them, they made this request of Him: "Lord, teach us to pray" (Luke 11:1).

Perhaps that is your request today. "*Lord, teach me to pray.*" In the previous chapter we looked at people in the Bible who prayed for a variety of reasons. Because prayer is simply communication with our Friend, our Father, our King, we can talk to Him about anything. That's what Jesus did—and He is our ultimate example.

While Jesus was on earth, He talked to His Father through prayer. They were in constant communication. Look at what the following verses tell us about Jesus' habit of prayer:

The next morning Jesus awoke long before daybreak and went out alone into the wilderness to pray. (Mark 1:35, NLT)

Afterward he went up into the hills by himself to pray. (Mark 6:46, NLT)

One day soon afterward Jesus went to a mountain to pray, and he prayed to God all night. (Luke 6:12, NLT)

Jesus took time to talk to His Father. He often went off alone, where He would not be distracted or interrupted. Prayer was a vital part of His time on this earth. If Jesus took the time to talk with His Father, how much more should we!

THE PRAYER JESUS TAUGHT HIS DISCIPLES

The prayer Jesus taught His disciples wasn't necessarily meant to be prayed verbatim, although there is nothing wrong with doing that. But just before He gave them this prayer He told them: "When you pray, don't use vain repetitions as the heathen do. For they think that they will be heard for their many words" (Matthew 6:7).

In other words, this prayer wasn't meant to be the only prayer they could ever pray—otherwise it would have become no more than vain repetition. Instead, it is a pattern for the way Jesus' followers can approach their heavenly Father in prayer. It is not what we have to pray, but a template that shows *how* we should pray.

Listen to what Jesus said:

This, then, is how you should pray: "Our Father in heaven, hallowed be your name, your kingdom come, your will be done on earth as it is in heaven. Give us today our daily bread. Forgive us our debts, as we also have forgiven our debtors. And lead us not into temptation, but deliver us from the evil one." (Matthew 6:9-13, NIV)

This prayer can be divided into two parts. The first deals with God's glory, the second with our needs. We will look at each phrase separately and discuss what it means regarding our own prayers.

"OUR FATHER IN HEAVEN, HALLOWED BE YOUR NAME...."

The beginning of this prayer is noteworthy. To call God "our Father" was a revolutionary thought to the disciples. As Jews, they feared God and attached such sacredness to His name that they wouldn't even utter it! But when Jesus went to the cross to die for our sins, He brought us back into a relationship with God. As He said to Mary Magdalene after His resurrection, "I am ascending to my Father and your Father, my God and your God" (John 20:17).

God is not some distant, unapproachable being. He wants to draw close to us, and He wants us to draw close to Him. The Bible tells us, "You should not be like cowering, fearful slaves. You should behave instead like God's very own children, adopted into his family—calling him 'Father, dear Father'" (Romans 8:15, NLT).

The word "hallowed" could also be translated *holy*. God is holy, meaning He is totally and completely perfect, separate from all that is sinful. Because we are sinful beings, there was no way for us to ever have a relationship with Him.

That's why Jesus had to come—as a human, but without sin—in order to bridge the gap between us and God. It is vital that we remember this awesome and holy God is also our loving Father. He can be both because of what Jesus did in taking our place on the cross and paying for our sins.

On the cross, God treated Jesus as if He had personally committed every sin ever committed by every person who would ever live—even though He had committed none of them. Because of this, His righteousness has been placed into our spiritual bank account.

As our loving heavenly Father, God has our best interests at heart. God is all-powerful, all-knowing, and present everywhere. That means He is unlimited in power, ignorant of nothing, and not bound by time or space. He is just, good, righteous, and loving. His decisions and purposes are always right and proper, always motivated by a pure goodness and a deep and abiding love for us.

The fact that you and I could even have the privilege of

approaching a God like this is staggering. Yet when Jesus instructed His disciples to pray, He didn't say, "Our God in heaven," but "Our *Father* in heaven." The all-powerful, all-knowing, present-everywhere, holy, righteous, good, and loving Creator of the entire universe is "our Father in heaven"!

Through the structure of this prayer, Jesus is showing us that when we pray, we should not immediately come to God with our wants or even our needs. Instead, we should first contemplate the greatness and glory of our Father.

"YOUR KINGDOM COME"

Contained in these words is a multilevel request with different shades of meaning. First of all, this is a request for Jesus' return to earth. The word that Jesus uses here for kingdom does not refer primarily to a geographical territory but to sovereignty and dominion. Therefore, when we pray "your kingdom come," we are praying for God's rule on earth, which essentially begins when Jesus returns to rule and reign.

The word come indicates a sudden, instantaneous coming. In essence, we're saying, "Lord, please come back…and do it soon!"

Is your spiritual life in such a place right now where you can pray this? The ability to truly say that you want Jesus to return is an indicator of where you are with God. The person who is walking with God daily will also be longing for His return.

A second aspect of this request is personal. When we say, "Your kingdom come," we are asking for the kingdom of God to come in our own lives. When Jesus walked the earth, He said, "The Kingdom of God has come upon you" (Matthew 12:28). He was referring to His presence.

As a new believer, you know that Jesus Himself has taken up residence in your life. When you pray this prayer, you're saying that you want Jesus to rule and reign in your life and that you want to live by the principles found in His Word. You want Him to be in charge; you're giving Him the master key to every room in your life.

When you pray "Your kingdom come," you're also praying "my kingdom go," for there can't be two kingdoms ruling in your life. Praying "Your kingdom come" is saying, "Lord, if what I am about to pray for is in any way outside of Your will, then overrule it."

Another facet of this phrase encompasses a request for the salvation of those who don't know the Lord. As His kingdom is ruling and reigning in our own lives, we can play a part in bringing it to others as well. God's kingdom is brought to this earth each time a new soul is brought to Jesus.

Seen in this way, "Your kingdom come" is also an evangelistic prayer. We are praying for the rule and reign of Jesus in the lives of many others. This is a reminder that we should be praying for the salvation of those who don't yet know the Lord.

"YOUR WILL BE DONE ON EARTH AS IT IS IN HEAVEN"

To want God's will to be done means that we need to seek to align our will with His. Then we will see our prayers answered in the affirmative. There is no doubt that it is the will of God that people come to believe in Jesus Christ. The Bible tells us, "[The Lord] does not want anyone to perish" (2 Peter 3:9, NLT). God's desire is to save people. Isaiah 53:12 (NLT) prophesies about Jesus that He "interceded for sinners." On the cross He prayed for His murderers, "Father, forgive these people, because they don't know what they are doing" (Luke 23:34, NLT).

A striking illustration of prayer for nonbelievers is shown in the story of Stephen, the first Christian martyr. The Jewish leaders stoned him to death because of his uncompromising stand for Jesus. Yet even as he was dying, he said, "Lord, don't hold this sin against them" (Acts 7:60, NIV).

The next chapter in Acts tells us that a young man was watching the execution that day—even holding the coats of those who were throwing the stones. His name was Saul (or, in Greek, Paul). He would soon become a Christian himself and would change the world for Christ.

That makes me wonder: Could Stephen, inspired by the Holy Spirit, have been praying specifically for Saul? When Saul became a Christian, it was such an astounding surprise that most people didn't believe it. Some even thought he was pretending to be converted in order to find even more Christians and turn them over to the Jewish leaders.

Clearly, God loves to save people—and He sometimes does it in the most amazing ways to the most surprising people. Do you know someone right now whom you cannot even imagine being a Christian? Start praying for that person! Pray for God's will to be done, on earth as it is in heaven. Pray that God's will—that all would be saved—will be made a reality in the life of this person.

Of course, the final outcome will lie with God, but it is certainly God's will that we pray this way.

"GIVE US TODAY OUR DAILY BREAD"

It's really amazing to consider that the all-knowing, all-powerful, present-everywhere God who created the entire universe could have any personal interest in us. Job wondered the same thing when he said, "What is man that you make so much of him, that you give him so much attention?" (Job 7:17, NIV).

Why would God be concerned about what concerns us? Why would He care about our needs—and even our wants? Why would He commit Himself personally to providing our "daily bread"?

Many reasons could be cited, but the most notable is simply that He loves us! Jesus told His followers, "Don't be afraid, little flock. For it gives your Father great happiness to give you the Kingdom" (Luke 12:32, NLT).

"Give us today our daily bread" is not only a request; it is also an affirmation that everything we have ultimately comes from God. James wrote, "Every good gift and every perfect gift is from above, and comes down from the Father of lights, with whom there is no variation or shadow of turning" (James 1:17).

Every good gift is from Him!

Yes, we can work hard, save, and wisely invest our money, but the very ability to do this comes from God. "It is He who gives you power to get wealth" (Deuteronomy 8:18).

In this prayer, Jesus gives us permission to ask God to provide for us—because everything we already have came from Him. God Almighty has committed Himself to personally meeting the needs of His children. The Bible assures us, "Since God didn't spare even his own Son but gave him up for us all, won't God, who gave us Christ, also give us everything else?" (Romans 8:32, NLT).

Of course, this doesn't mean that we can sit around like lazy bums and say, "Give me my daily bread, Lord!" The Bible also says that those who don't work shouldn't eat (see 2 Thessalonians 3:10). We must be diligent to do our part, working hard, putting in an honest day's work. To pray for God's provision of our daily bread is to recognize God as the Provider, even as we work for our bread. We do our part, and God promises to do His.

"FORGIVE US OUR DEBTS, AS WE ALSO HAVE FORGIVEN OUR DEBTORS"

I once heard of a minister who, short of time and unable to find a parking space, left his car in a "no parking" zone. He put a note under the windshield wiper that read, "I have circled the block ten times. I have an appointment to keep. 'Forgive us our debts.'"

When he returned, he found a citation from a police officer along with this note: "I've circled this block for ten years. If I don't give you a ticket, I could lose my job. 'Lead us not into temptation.'"

What are our "debts"? The word translated debts could also be translated as sins, trespasses, shortcomings, resentments, what we owe to someone, or a wrong we've done.

Some people think they don't need forgiveness. But according to this model prayer, forgiveness is something we should request on a regular basis. "If we say we have no sin, we are only fooling ourselves and refusing to accept the truth" (1 John 1:8, NLT). People who don't see a constant need for regular cleansing from sin are not spending much time in God's presence.

Of course, when you accepted Jesus as your Savior, He washed away all your sin and freed you from its stranglehold. However, while you are still in this life, you will battle with your sin nature. The greater the saint, the greater is the sense of sin and the awareness of sin within. The great apostle Paul described the battle with these words:

> I don't understand myself at all, for I really want to do what is right, but I don't do it. Instead, I do the very thing I hate. I know perfectly well that what I am doing is wrong, and my bad conscience shows that I agree that the law is good. But I can't help myself, because it is sin inside me that makes me do these evil things. I know I am rotten through and through so far as my old sinful nature is concerned. No matter which way I turn, I can't make myself do right. I want to, but I can't. When I want to do good, I don't. And when I try not to do wrong, I do it anyway. But if I am doing what I don't want to do, I am not really the one doing it; the sin within me is doing it. It seems to be a fact of life that when I want to do what is right, I inevitably do what is wrong. (Romans 7:15-21, NLT)

Is that how you feel sometimes? If so, welcome to the human race! The fact is, your sin nature is still very much a part of you. You will continue to sin, but you can always come to God for forgiveness and cleansing.

Because we have been forgiven, we should willingly extend forgiveness to others. Think about how many movies and TV programs you have seen where the basic premise is this: the good guy gets hurt, the good guy regroups, the good guy pulverizes the bad guy.

When is the last time you saw a program where the good guy gets hurt and then forgives the bad guy? Are you kidding? It doesn't happen! Society doesn't seem to take kindly to forgiveness. It values vengeance instead. In our culture we firmly believe the adage, "Don't get mad, get even!"

As fatally flawed people, we are going to sin. We are going to hurt one another, whether intentionally or unintentionally. But according to Jesus, forgiven people should be forgiving people. In many ways, forgiveness is the key to all relationships that are healthy, strong, and lasting.

Jesus was speaking on the topic of forgiveness when Peter asked, "'Lord, how often should I forgive someone who sins against me? Seven times?' 'No!' Jesus replied, 'seventy times seven!'" (Matthew 18:21-22, NLT).

Peter had really thought he was being generous to offer to forgive someone seven times. But Jesus said that we should be willing to forgive 490 times!

In other words, don't even keep count! Just keep on forgiving. The number of times the other person sins is the number of times you should forgive.

"But," you may protest, "the person doesn't deserve forgiveness!"

Did you deserve to be forgiven by God?

That's right. You don't deserve forgiveness either. But God forgave you anyway. That's the kind of forgiveness Jesus expects us to extend to others. Paul put it this way: "Be kind to each other, tenderhearted, forgiving one another, just as God through Christ has forgiven you" (Ephesians 4:32, NLT).

"LEAD US NOT INTO TEMPTATION, BUT DELIVER US FROM THE EVIL ONE"

This phrase doesn't mean that God ever would lead us into temptation. In fact, the Bible also says, "Remember, no one who wants to do wrong should ever say, 'God is tempting me.' God is never tempted to do wrong, and he never tempts anyone else either. Temptation comes from the lure of our own evil desires. These evil desires lead to evil actions, and evil actions lead to death" (James 1:13-15, NLT).

When we pray for God not to lead us into temptation, we are asking God to guide us so that we won't get out of His will and place ourselves in the way of temptation. We're saying, "Lord, don't let me be tempted above my capacity to resist."

Temptation itself is not a sin. Jesus Himself was tempted, and Jesus never sinned. Our problem with temptation, of course, is that we can rationalize giving in to it. Sometimes we don't see temptation for what it is until it's too late. That's where we need God's help—and that's why we need to pray these words.

If we could see our own temptations as clearly as we see other people's, they wouldn't be that hard to identify. Other people's temptations look so ugly and foolish that we say, "How could they do that?" Yet somehow ours seem different, acceptable, justifiable. We think, "My case is different."

Then one day our house of cards collapses, and we see our sin for what it really is.

Here's a litmus test to apply when you are not sure if something is a temptation (an enticement to evil). First, pray about it and bring it into the clear light of God's presence. When you're not sure, ask, "Should I allow myself to be in this potentially vulnerable situation? Lord, if this is not pleasing to you, let me know, and I'll get out of here!"

If you find that you really *don't* want to pray about something, chances are you already know the answer. When you are following your Father in heaven, who is holy (as acknowledged at the beginning of this prayer), then you will begin to see things as they really are.

A second thing you should do is ask yourself, "How would this look if some other Christian gave in to it?" If you saw another Christian doing what you are thinking of doing, how would you react? You see, God knows how dangerous temptation is. It is so—well—tempting! Satan knows that if he can just give us a taste, he can get us hooked. It's like trying to eat just one potato chip or one freshly baked cookie.

So we need God to help us steer clear of temptation.

What makes resisting temptation difficult for many people is that they don't try to avoid it completely. They want to be delivered from temptation without giving up the very things that put them in the path of temptation. To pray for protection against temptation and then rush into places of vulnerability is to thrust your fingers into the fire and hope they don't get burnt.

When Jesus told us to pray this way, He wanted us to always have before us our vulnerability to temptation and our need for vigilance. When we pray "lead us not into temptation," we are saying, "Lord, I know my own sinful vulnerabilities, and I ask you to keep me from the power of sin. Help me to make the right choices and avoid anything that would pull me away from you."

This is an appeal to God to watch over our eyes, our ears, our mouth, our feet, our hands. We are asking that in whatever we see, hear, or say, in any place we go, and in anything we do, He will protect us from sin. We are laying claim to the promise recorded in 1 Corinthians 10:13 (NLT):

> Remember that the temptations that come into your life are no different from what others experience. And God is faithful. He will keep the temptation from becoming so strong that you can't stand up against it. When you are tempted, he will show you a way out so that you won't give in to it.

This part of the Lord's Prayer is asking God to show us that "way out." Jesus taught that we should always approach God recognizing His awesome greatness. We should worship and adore Him. We should pray for His perfect will and the rule of His kingdom in our lives and in the lives of others. Then, after getting things into the proper perspective, we should bring our personal needs before Him.

EIGHT
CONVERSING WITH GOD

I heard a story of a woman in Florida who fended off a would-be rapist with the Lord's Prayer. When she was attacked, she began to recite the words of that prayer in rapid-fire fashion. Her attacker covered his face with his hands and started shaking. As she repeated the prayer, he let her go and fled.

Later the woman said that a peace came over her as she started praying the Lord's Prayer. She prayed to be delivered from evil, and she was!

HOW TO PRAY

The Lord's Prayer is a powerful prayer. You should seek to memorize and use it, but remember that it shouldn't be the only prayer you ever pray.

In chapter 7 we examined the meaning of each phrase. But how do you use this prayer as a pattern for your private time with the Lord?

I once learned a helpful acronym that can remind us how to pray. (Of course, God listens to all of our prayers—even the ones that don't follow this pattern!)

The word is ACTS, and the letters stand for

Adoration

Confession

Thanksgiving

Supplication

ADORATION

As in the Lord's Prayer, you can begin your prayer time by "adoring" God. This helps you remember that God is not a cosmic vending machine but deserves to be approached with reverence and awe.

Maybe you think you don't have a whole lot to say, but start by acknowledging His greatness, power, and majesty. As the psalmist said, "Oh, magnify the LORD with me, and let us exalt His name together" (Psalm 34:3).

When we see God for who He is, we begin to see our problems for what they are. In the book of Acts, the believers were told they could no longer preach the gospel. Instead of cowering in fear, they prayed. And they began their prayer by worshiping God and reflecting on His Word, thereby putting their considerable problems into the proper perspective:

> Then all the believers were united as they lifted their voices in prayer: "O Sovereign Lord, Creator of heaven and earth, the sea, and everything in them—you spoke long ago by the Holy Spirit through our ancestor King David, your servant, saying, 'Why did the nations rage? Why did the people waste their time with futile plans? The kings of the earth prepared for battle; the rulers gathered

together against the Lord and against his Messiah.' That is what has happened here in this city! For Herod Antipas, Pontius Pilate the governor, the Gentiles, and the people of Israel were all united against Jesus, your holy servant, whom you anointed. In fact, everything they did occurred according to your eternal will and plan." (Acts 4:24-28, NLT)

Having considered all that God had done in the past, they came to the problem at hand.

And now, O Lord, hear their threats, and give your servants great boldness in their preaching. Send your healing power; may miraculous signs and wonders be done through the name of your holy servant Jesus. After this prayer, the building where they were meeting shook, and they were all filled with the Holy Spirit. And they preached God's message with boldness. (Acts 4:29-31, NLT)

They began their prayer with adoration, got their problem into perspective, then made their request with boldness. And God answered!

CONFESSION

When you became a Christian, Jesus washed away all your sin. But you will soon discover (if you haven't already) that you still commit sin. The difference now is that you have an avenue for forgiveness in your relationship with God. When you come to Him in prayer, truly acknowledging and adoring Him, you will become painfully aware of your own weakness and vulnerability.

You need to take your sins to God and let Him forgive them. You see, if your relationship with God is like a fine piece of machinery, then sin is like a grain of sand that gets in and mucks up the gears. To pray for God's will to be done and to be in tune with what He wants, you need to deal with sin on a daily basis.

The great thing is this: God promises that when we confess, He forgives—always:

> If we confess our sins, he is faithful and just and will forgive us our sins and purify us from all unrighteousness.
> (1 John 1:9, NIV)

Besides, confession is good for us:

> Finally, I confessed all my sins to you and stopped trying to hide them. I said to myself, "I will confess my rebellion to the LORD." And you forgave me! All my guilt is gone.
> (Psalm 32:5, NLT)

That's why confession is so vital in your relationship with God. Ask God to show you any wrongs that need to be cleansed. Maybe you already know them—tell God. He already knows anyway, and He promises to forgive.

THANKSGIVING

This is just what it sounds like. So often when we pray, we have a list of things we want God to do. However, if we follow the ACTS pattern, we first think about everything God has already done. Before you present your requests, what can you thank God for?

Look again at Paul and Silas, praising God before God's deliverance came:

> They were severely beaten, and then they were thrown into prison. The jailer was ordered to make sure they didn't escape. So he took no chances but put them into the inner dungeon and clamped their feet in the stocks. Around midnight, Paul and Silas were praying and singing hymns to God, and the other prisoners were listening.
> (Acts 16:23-25, NLT)

How could they do such a thing under such difficult circumstances? They weren't necessarily in a position where one might think about being thankful, but they did it anyway. They knew that even in that awful dungeon they were right in the center of God's will. So they thanked Him for being with them.

Prayers of thanks were a part of Old Testament leader Nehemiah's lifestyle too. (You'll learn more about him later in this chapter.) When the people were rebuilding the walls of Jerusalem, he led them in prayers and songs of thankfulness to God:

> I led the leaders of Judah to the top of the wall and organized two large choirs to give thanks. . . .The two choirs that were giving thanks then proceeded to the Temple of God, where they took their places. So did I, together with the group of leaders who were with me. (Nehemiah 12:31, 40, NLT)

So after you've adored God and confessed your sin, take a few minutes for "T"—Thanksgiving. You'll discover so many things to be thankful for, and you'll be humbled to realize all that God has done and is doing for you every day.

SUPPLICATION

This is really just a fancy word for asking, but it also includes the elements of humility and honesty. And once you've adored God, confessed your sin, and thanked Him for all He has done for you, how could you be anything other than humble and honest? Your requests will naturally come from a humble heart.

It may help you to keep a list of ongoing prayer requests—things you want to pray about. Some people have prayer notebooks divided into the days of the week. They spread their regular requests (such as prayers for family and friends) across those days so each request gets made once a week.

It is also helpful to keep a written list of special prayer requests.

In one column write the date you start praying for a specific request, and in another column write the date of God's answer. It may seem strange now, but over time you'll begin to see a whole column of requests and a whole column of answers.

This becomes a strong encouragement to continue to pray for your own needs and the needs of others.

These verses from the Psalms may also encourage you:

> The LORD has heard my supplication,
> the LORD receives my prayer.
> (Psalm 6:9, NASB)

> I love the LORD, because He hears my voice and
> my supplications.
> (Psalm 116:1, NASB)

> Let my supplication come before You;
> deliver me according to Your word.
> (Psalm 119:170, NASB)

Wind up your prayer with supplication, presenting your requests to God. He will receive your prayer, hear your voice, and deliver you, just as His Word promises.

ATTITUDES FOR PRAYER

The communication you have with God should be like the communication you have with a friend—direct, honest, frequent. Yet unlike a friend, God is never too sensitive for our questions or too busy to talk to us or too sentimental to tell us what we may need to hear. We can pray about anything, anytime, with confidence and boldness, knowing that God will answer.

BE HONEST

If you ever think you can hide something from God, you're in for a big surprise. He knows you completely. He knows your fears, your weaknesses, your strengths, your worries. No matter how you appear to others on the outside, God knows your motives.

When Jesus was in the garden of Gethsemane facing the most difficult hours of His earthly life, He asked His disciples to pray. He knew that He needed strength for the coming hours, but He knew they needed it too. And it was strength that could not possibly come from within themselves but would have to come from God. So He said to them, "Pray that you won't be overcome by temptation" (Luke 22:40, NLT).

For the disciples, the temptation would be to run away, to deny ever knowing anything about Jesus—temptation they pretty much all gave in to one way or another.

But Jesus' advice is helpful for all of us on a daily basis. You will face temptation—being a believer doesn't make it any less tempting; in fact, sometimes temptation seems even more powerful. God knows your weaknesses—maybe better than you do. He wants you to pray to Him when you are faced with temptation to sin.

Remember, you can be completely honest with God. You might as well—He already knows everything anyway. So when you face a difficult situation, ask God to help you not to be overcome.

TELL GOD EVERYTHING

Another important verse to learn about prayer comes from Paul's letter to the Philippians. Most people focus on the word worry in this verse but the word pray is just as important:

> Don't worry about anything; instead, pray about everything. Tell God what you need, and thank him for all he has done. (Philippians 4:6, NLT)

"Pray about everything." Did you know you can do that? You can talk to God about anything and everything.

The book of Nehemiah gives us a great study on the power and procedure of prayer. Nehemiah was cupbearer to the king of Persia. His family had been taken into exile, and Nehemiah had risen to this trusted position.

Yet Nehemiah longed for Jerusalem. Like many other Jews, he missed living in their land and worshiping in their temple.

We read in Nehemiah 1:5-11 (NLT) a prayer he prayed upon receiving the news about the broken-down walls of the city of Jerusalem:

> Then I said, "O LORD, God of heaven, the great and awesome God who keeps his covenant of unfailing love with those who love him and obey his commands, listen to my prayer! Look down and see me praying night and day for your people Israel. I confess that we have sinned against you. Yes, even my own family and I have sinned! We have sinned terribly by not obeying the commands, laws, and regulations that you gave us through your servant Moses.

> "Please remember what you told your servant Moses: 'If you sin, I will scatter you among the nations. But if you return to me and obey my commands, even if you are exiled to the ends of the earth, I will bring you back to the place I have chosen for my name to be honored.'

> "We are your servants, the people you rescued by your great power and might. O Lord, please hear my prayer! Listen to the prayers of those of us who delight in honoring you. Please grant me success now as I go to ask the king for a great favor. Put it into his heart to be kind to me."

Notice the pattern of Nehemiah's prayer. Although he was weeping, his first words glorify and acknowledge God (just as in the Lord's Prayer). Notice the confession of sin on behalf of his people. Then finally, at the end, he presents his request. And what a request!

He was going to ask the king for a leave of absence from his job as cupbearer to go to Jerusalem and head up the rebuilding of the city's walls. This was quite a sacrifice on Nehemiah's part.

A cupbearer had access to the king and was in a position of influence and power. Yet the people of God needed help, and Nehemiah was in a position to do something. So he did!

Then notice something else. Nehemiah is still grieving, trying to figure out what to do, when the king notices that he looks sad and asks him about it.

The Bible says that Nehemiah "was badly frightened" (Nehemiah 2:2, NLT). Why? Well, in that culture the king could have a person killed for just looking sad in his presence. But what did Nehemiah do? He swallowed hard, and then explained precisely and respectfully just why he was sad. The king offered to help, and "with a prayer to the God of heaven" (v. 4, NLT), Nehemiah spelled out his request (he'd obviously thought this through very carefully).

Nehemiah gives us an example of a long prayer in a time of deep conversation with God and a quick prayer in a time of immediate need. Nehemiah could pray a quick prayer because he already had a foundation of fervent and honest prayer to God.

Tell God everything when you pray. Tell God the big needs and the little needs. Spend time with God in lengthy conversations and then you'll be able to send up short SOS prayers at a moment's notice. God is always listening, so always pray!

NEVER GIVE UP

How important it is that we learn the value of praying *persistently*. Some say you should only pray about something once—to pray about it again would show a lack of faith. I don't believe this is what Scripture teaches us.

In fact, I think the Bible teaches the opposite approach.

Before He went to the cross, Jesus prayed more than once, "Let this cup of suffering be taken away from me" (Matthew 26:39, 42, 44, NLT).

The apostle Paul prayed three times for the Lord to heal an illness that seemed to be curtailing his ministry (see 2 Corinthians 12:8).

In Luke 18:1-8 (NLT) Jesus told a parable highlighting this important aspect of prayer:

> One day Jesus told his disciples a story to illustrate their need for constant prayer and to show them that they must never give up. "There was a judge in a certain city," he said, "who was a godless man with great contempt for everyone. A widow of that city came to him repeatedly, appealing for justice against someone who had harmed her. The judge ignored her for a while, but eventually she wore him out. 'I fear neither God nor man,' he said to himself, 'but this woman is driving me crazy. I'm going to see that she gets justice, because she is wearing me out with her constant requests!'"

> Then the Lord said, "Learn a lesson from this evil judge. Even he rendered a just decision in the end, so don't you think God will surely give justice to his chosen people who plead with him day and night? Will he keep putting them off? I tell you, he will grant justice to them quickly! But when I, the Son of Man, return, how many will I find who have faith?

In 1 Thessalonians 5:17-18 we are reminded to "pray without ceasing, in everything give thanks; for this is the will of God in Christ Jesus for you".

Sometimes God's timing is not ours. In fact, often God's timing is not ours. Even so, we should be persistent—pray without ceasing. God never gets tired of hearing our requests; He never leaves the answering machine on to screen out our persistent calls. He encourages us to keep on praying, always trusting that He will answer in His way, in His time.

BE BOLD AND CONFIDENT

The apostle James tell us not to doubt that God will answer our prayers:

> If you need wisdom—if you want to know what God wants you to do—ask him, and he will gladly tell you. He won't resent your asking. But when you ask him, be sure that you really expect him to answer, for a doubtful mind is as unsettled as a wave of the sea that is driven and tossed by the wind. People like that should not expect to receive anything from the Lord. They can't make up their minds. They waver back and forth in everything they do. (James 1:5-8, NLT)

You may feel new at this, but don't worry. Right from the start, pray with confidence. There is nothing wrong with being bold and confident in your prayers. In fact, you *should* be.

Jesus gave His followers these promises about prayer:

> Listen to me! You can pray for anything, and if you believe, you will have it. (Mark 11:24, NLT)

> I also tell you this: If two of you agree down here on earth concerning anything you ask, my Father in heaven will do it for you. (Matthew 18:19, NLT)

So, you might be wondering, I can pray for lots of money, and it will come? I can pray to win that promotion or get into that school or get a new car, and it will just happen? I can pray for someone to be healed, and he will be healed? I can pray about anything, and if I believe, I will get it?

Well, yes and no.

As with any verse of Scripture, you always have to read all that Jesus said on the topic—not taking your entire theology from one verse. And then you must always read what is said before and after that verse. It's called "reading in context."

As a new believer, you will grow in your knowledge of God by reading His Word. The more you learn about Him, the more you'll understand what the Bible calls "the mind of Christ." You'll seek God's desires above your own when you pray. After all, you may think that what you desire is the very best thing—but God may have other plans.

NINE
EXPECTING GOD'S ANSWERS

God has promised to answer our prayers—but He's never said the answer will always be yes! As human beings we will never be able to fathom God and His ways. He sees the big picture; He knows what good can come out of bad situations; He knows certain bad things need to come to strengthen our character or prepare us for a future task. So even when we pray for what we think is God's will, we need to allow God to do His work, in His way, in His time.

WHEN GOD SAYS "NO"

Sometimes, no matter how well-intentioned your prayer, God will say no. That happened to Paul. This great apostle traveled across much of the Roman Empire, fearlessly taking the gospel into cities where he was laughed at, beaten, jailed, and once even stoned and left for dead.

Paul, however, had a problem.

It was a very serious problem.

In fact, the apostle called it a "thorn in [the] flesh" (2 Corinthians 12:7). We don't know for sure what the problem was. Some commentators believe it had to do with his eyes, because when he wrote to the Galatians he said, "I know you would gladly have taken out your own eyes and given them to me if it had been possible" (Galatians 4:15, NLT).

Paul had an entire world he wanted to reach for Christ. Doesn't it make sense that he would pray for God to take his disability away so he could be even more effective in his ministry?

It was a prayer that "made perfect sense" and certainly it seemed to Paul, was in line with God's will. His motivation in asking for healing was so he could be more effective in ministry.

But God still said no.

Each time He said, "My gracious favor is all you need. My power works best in your weakness" (2 Corinthians 12:9, NLT).

God made it clear that He knew better than Paul. What was the reason? Paul explained that one reason was to keep him from getting too proud. His "thorn" reminded him that everything he accomplished was by God's grace and strength.

Maybe another reason was that God knew His busy messenger needed rest once in a while—and he'd only take it if it was forced on him. Whatever the case, God knew best, and His answer was no.

WHEN GOD SAYS "WAIT"

Sometimes you will get a yes, but the answer may not be visible for many years—in essence, you are getting a "wait."

For example, God may say, "Yes, I will bring that person into My kingdom," but you may wait many years to see it happen.

Time, we need to remember, is very different with God. The Bible says, "You must not forget, dear friends, that a day is like a thousand years to the Lord, and a thousand years is like a day" (2 Peter 3:8, NLT). So you may be waiting for years and years while, according to God, He answered the very day you asked!

The "wait" answer can be very difficult because we want to see results. At times we think that God just didn't hear us. But remember the parable Jesus taught about prayer. He said keep on praying; never give up; be persistent.

Sometimes the answer God gives is totally unexpected. Look at the example of Zechariah, father of John the Baptist. Zechariah served as a priest in Israel.

Back in Old Testament times, King David had made up a schedule so priests from all over Israel could come for a couple of weeks at a time to serve in God's temple in Jerusalem. One priest was chosen by lot (like drawing straws) to actually enter the Holy Place in the temple to burn incense each morning. This was a great honor and probably a once-in-a-lifetime opportunity.

Well, one particular morning when Zechariah's division (called the Abijah division) was on duty, the lot fell to Zechariah. "As was the custom of the priests, he was chosen by lot to enter the sanctuary and burn incense in the Lord's presence" (Luke 1:9, NLT).

So he went into the Holy Place, and an angel appeared and said, "Don't be afraid, Zechariah! For God has heard your prayer, and your wife, Elizabeth, will bear you a son! And you are to name him John" (Luke 1:13, NLT).

What did the angel mean? Was Zechariah in the Holy Place praying for his wife to have a son? I doubt it. Most likely he was praying for the promised Messiah to come and deliver his nation—that would be the appropriate prayer for a priest who entered the Holy Place. But surely Zechariah had prayed many, many times that he and Elizabeth would have a child.

Since the Bible tells us they were old and well past the age of childbearing, my guess is that they had stopped praying that prayer some time ago.

Now, unexpectedly, after years of thinking God was saying no, Zechariah and Elizabeth realized that His answer had really been "wait." He had finally said yes to their prayer for a child. And at the same time, God was also answering the prayer for the coming of the Messiah, for which Zechariah and the people in the temple were probably praying (see Luke 1:10).

The coming of Zechariah's child was one link in the answer to the prayers of an entire nation, for that child, John the Baptist, would be the messenger to announce the Messiah.

God will answer your prayers, but many times His answers will surprise you. Often they will be so much better than you could have dreamed up yourself. Sometimes you'll sense a touch of humor in His answers. And you'll discover that His timing was much better than the timing you had wanted.

When you pray, be ready! The answers may come in the most unexpected ways.

JOINED TO JESUS

Jesus gave us an incredible promise about answering prayer:

> If you stay joined to me and my words remain in you, you may ask any request you like, and it will be granted! (John 15:7, NLT)

Literally, Jesus was saying, "I command you to ask at once for yourselves whatsoever you desire. It's yours."

Quite a promise! But there are some conditions in that promise: "If you stay joined to me and my words remain in you." What does this mean? To be "joined" to Jesus means to be living in continual fellowship with Him, like two friends who are comfortable in each other's presence. You are not ill at ease, looking forward to getting away from Him; instead, you look forward to being together, and you enjoy each other's company.

This is what Jesus was implying when He said, "Look! Here I stand at the door and knock. If you hear me calling and open the door, I will come in, and we will share a meal as friends" (Revelation 3:20, NLT).

Being joined to Jesus pictures intimate friendship. That means that everything you do and every choice you make revolves around Jesus. It means that He has a say in everything you do. It means that you seek always to glorify Him in your life.

Remember that this intimacy must be balanced with a healthy reverence and awe of who God is. We are not to become too cavalier with God, either.

I live in southern California—the capital of casual. Many people carry their casual outlook toward life into the church, their relationship with God, and their prayer lives. God is almighty, and He is to be revered, worshiped, and obeyed. The way you live has a lot to do with how your prayers are answered.

If you are practicing a sin, your prayers will go nowhere. Notice that I didn't say, "If you ever sin, your prayers will go nowhere." No— of course you will sin every day. But if you are holding on to something that you know is a sin, and you refuse to stop doing it, you can't expect God to answer your prayers. Why not? Because if you aren't listening to what He has already told you, He's not going to say any more to you. The psalmist says, "If I had cherished sin in my heart, the Lord would not have listened" (Psalm 66:18, NIV).

When you're joined to Jesus, you will always seek to glorify Him, to put Him first in everything. There is a story in the Bible of a man who came to Jesus and wanted to follow Him. But the man said, "Lord, first let me return home and bury my father" (Matthew 8:21, NLT).

The wrong here is not that the man needed to attend a funeral; the point is that he wanted to follow Jesus, but not until his father had passed away. Maybe he was afraid if he took off with Jesus, he'd lose his inheritance or his reputation or whatever.

To say "Lord" and then "first let me" is an oxymoron. (You know what that is, don't you? That's when words that are actually opposites are put together, like…jumbo shrimp, genuine imitation, or freezer burn.)

Many people have the attitude that they can follow God tomorrow or when it's more convenient. But if you're joined to Christ, you can't say "me first"; this must be reflected in your prayers.

Your prayers are not a grocery list of things you need or want; if they were, you might as well pray to "our Santa in heaven" or "our butler in heaven." No, your prayers are part of your relationship with God.

Prayer is two-way communication: you talk; you listen. Chances are, God will say a whole lot more to you than you might have thought! Prayer is about being joined to Jesus. It's about putting Him first.

HIS WORD IN YOU

In the second part of John 15:7 (NLT), Jesus says, "[If] my words remain in you, you may ask any request you like, and it will be granted!"

What does this mean about your prayers?

To have God's words remain in you means that God's Word is at home in your heart. This means, therefore, that your prayers cannot be divorced from your lifestyle. Your prayers flow out of a close walk with God. If your life is not pleasing to God, your prayer life will be ineffective, inconsistent, and maybe even nonexistent.

Obedience plays an important part in answered prayers:

> We will receive whatever we request because we obey him and do the things that please him. (1 John 3:22, NLT)

In other words, if we give a listening ear to all God's commands to us, He will give a listening ear to all our prayers to Him.

A big part of this is understanding to whom you are praying. The best way to learn more about God is to read His Word—the entire Bible—and see who He is and what He has done.

Read in Genesis how He created this beautiful world. Watch how sin enters the picture and how God immediately sets into place a plan to deal with it. See how He chose a man—Abraham—to be the father of a nation through whom the Messiah, the Savior, would come. Read about all the people in Genesis who disappointed God but through whom God continued to work because of His promise. And watch how He changed their lives. Imperfect people; a perfect God. God has a plan that stretches from eternity past to eternity future. God knows everything.

Read in Exodus the story of great evil in the world in the form of an Egyptian pharaoh who subdued God's people and killed their children. Watch God miraculously setting His people free from slavery—first wreaking havoc in the land of the Egyptians by showing each of their gods to be powerless. (The sun god cannot stop the darkness; the god of the Nile cannot keep the river from turning to blood; the god of the cattle cannot keep them from dying.) *God is all powerful.*

Study the laws God gave to His nation so that they could live in harmony with Him and with each other. *God is perfect and holy.*

Watch these imperfect people, just set free from slavery, complaining about living in the desert and wanting to go back to Egypt! Watch God deal kindly with them again and again; watch Him exact punishment when it is deserved. Sin has consequences, and *God is a just judge.*

Read about the Israelites finally receiving the land God promised to Abraham. God keeps His promises. *God is faithful.*

Read about the glory days under David and Solomon. Read the tragic stories of the kings. Study the prophets who consistently brought God's messages to the people during the time of the kings—some were listened to, most weren't. Yet God in His love sent warnings to His people, second chances (and third and fourth). *God is compassionate.*

Read about how God's Son came to earth to die for people—to take away the punishment our sins deserve. *God is love.*

Study the letters of the New Testament that show Christianity in action. Learn how to make your faith work in your daily life. *God is good.*

Absorb the book of Revelation that gives a glimpse of the future. One day, sin and evil will be completely vanquished and God's people will live with Him forever. *God is supreme and sovereign.*

The more you learn about God, the more you'll understand the Power to whom you are praying. When you think of the "bigness" of God, you will see the "smallness" of your problems in comparison. As Scripture says, "Is anything too hard for the LORD?" (Genesis 18:14).

When God's Word remains in you—that is, as you study and learn more about God and His workings with His people—you'll understand how to obey Him. With His Word in your heart, you'll know how to pray, and you can trust God to answer.

GOOD GIFTS

"Okay," you say, "I trust that God will answer, but I'm afraid of what He might say!" Many people are afraid that if they say to God, "I trust you with my life; I'll serve you completely," God will immediately send them to the place they least want to go—the deepest jungles of Africa, perhaps.

But let's look at what Jesus says:

"Keep on asking, and you will be given what you ask for. Keep on looking, and you will find. Keep on knocking, and the door will be opened. For everyone who asks, receives. Everyone who seeks, finds. And the door is opened to everyone who knocks. You parents—if your children ask for a loaf of bread, do you give them a stone instead? Or if they ask for a fish, do you give them a snake? Of course not! If you sinful people know how to give good gifts to your children, how much more will your heavenly Father give good gifts to those who ask him. (Matthew 7:7-11, NLT)

When your beautiful child comes to you and asks for a sandwich for lunch, you're not going to serve up poisonous snakes and think it's a big joke. And you're just a sinful human being! You love your children, so you try to always do what's best; you'd never intentionally hurt them or put them in danger.

Well, God is your perfect heavenly Father. When you come to Him with your humble heart, desiring to serve Him, He's not going to make you suffer as part of some big cosmic joke. He wants to make use of every gift He's given you—as well as your background, your experiences, what you enjoy—and wrap them into a big gift called your future.

Sure, He may send you in some unexpected directions, but you'll discover that serving Him will be your greatest fulfillment. You'll do things you never dreamed you could do; you'll accomplish for God acts that you never would have imagined. How? Because you let God work through you to build His kingdom.

Listen to God's declaration of His love for you:

> For I know the thoughts that I think toward you, says the Lord, thoughts of peace and not of evil, to give you a future and a hope. Then you will call upon Me and go and pray to Me, and I will listen to you. And you will seek Me and find Me, when you search for Me with all your heart. I will be found by you, says the Lord. (Jeremiah 29:11-14)

God's plans for you are good, not bad. He has a particular goal in mind for you. Take the time to contemplate His glory and character. Spend time in His presence through prayer. Begin to walk in His unique and wonderful plan for your life.

It will be the adventure of a lifetime!

TEN
IF GOD ALREADY KNOWS...WHY PRAY?

Now that's a really good question.

One of the first things you have learned about God is the fact that He is omniscient—meaning He knows everything. He knows the past, He knows the future, He knows your deepest, hidden (or so you thought) motives and desires. He knows your worries and fears. He knows your words before you say them. As the psalmist said:

> O LORD, you have examined my heart and know everything about me. You know when I sit down or stand up. You know my every thought when far away…You know what I am going to say even before I say it, LORD….You saw me before I was born. Every day of my life was recorded in your book. Every moment was laid out before a single day had passed. (Psalm 139:1-2, 4, 16, NLT)

And consider Jesus' words:

"Your Father knows exactly what you need even before you ask him!" (Matthew 6:8, NLT)

Well then…if God already knows what you're going to say, if He knows your needs before you ask, if He already knows what's going to happen anyway—then why bother to pray?

PRAY BECAUSE JESUS TOLD YOU TO

When Jesus was on earth, He prayed to His Father—even though His Father obviously already knew everything He would need.

In the garden of Gethsemane, Jesus spoke directly to God, pleading for Him to take away the cup of suffering, yet willing to complete the task God had given Him (see Mark 14:36; Luke 22:42). Before Jesus raised Lazarus from the dead, He first spoke to God:

Jesus looked up to heaven and said, "Father, thank you for hearing me. You always hear me, but I said it out loud for the sake of all these people standing here, so they will believe you sent me." Then Jesus shouted, "Lazarus, come out!" (John 11:41-43, NLT).

When Jesus fed the five thousand, He collected a small amount of food from a young boy, "looked up toward heaven, and asked God's blessing on the food. Breaking the loaves into pieces, he gave some of the bread and fish to each disciple, and the disciples gave them to the people" (Matthew 14:19, NLT).

Some mothers brought their children to Jesus, "so he could lay his hands on them and pray for them" (Matthew 19:13, NLT).

Jesus didn't pray in order to impress people; in fact, that was one of the problems He saw with the religious leaders. Jesus seemed to take it for granted that He needed to pray to God in order to receive His answers.

If it was that way for Jesus, it is most certainly the case with us!

Yes, we should pray simply because Jesus told us to. Even if it were extremely difficult to do (which it's not), or very unpleasant (which it isn't), or if we never got answers (which we do), we should pray because we are commanded to pray.

PRAY BECAUSE IT'S GOD'S PLAN FOR YOU

It is important to remember that prayer is not about changing God; it's about changing you! It's not about having to plead with God, wrestle with Him, instruct Him, or bend His arm to help you when He really doesn't want to. No, prayer is about talking to a God who truly cares about you. He wants to help you.

True praying is not overcoming God's reluctance but laying hold of His willingness! Martin Luther said, "By our praying, we are instructing ourselves more than Him."

Prayer is God's appointed way for obtaining things. The Bible says, "The reason you don't have what you want is that you don't ask God for it" (James 4:2, NLT).

You might ask, "Why is it that I don't seem to know God's will for my life?"

"The reason you don't have what you want is that you don't ask God for it."

"Why am I still struggling so much with certain sins?"

"The reason you don't have what you want is that you don't ask God for it."

"Why do I still face so many job and financial worries?"

"The reason you don't have what you want is that you don't ask God for it."

Jesus came that we might be able to have a relationship with His Father. Sin separated us from God, but Jesus died in our place, thereby satisfying the righteous demand of a holy God against whom we all have sinned.

As we realize that truth, turn from our sin, and put our faith in Jesus Christ as our Savior and Lord, we become God's children. And an integral part of our new relationship with God includes communication.

We don't have relationships with people we never talk to. A true relationship includes some give-and-take. Sometimes we talk and they listen, and sometimes it's the other way around. But we wouldn't have a relationship with someone who only talked or only listened. It has to be a two-way street.

Likewise, in order to have a relationship with God, you need to communicate with Him. The only way to communicate is through prayer. That will often include asking, because we are frail human beings who desperately need God's help in order to live our lives in ways that please Him.

Communication also means listening. What does it mean to "listen" to God? How do you do that? In order to hear God, you need to learn to tune in to what He is saying. Jesus often said, "If anyone has ears to hear, let him hear" (Mark 4:23, NIV).

It would be a great idea to somehow get away to a quiet place, as Jesus often did, retreat from the noisy crowds, and wait on the Father in prayer. It could also be as simple as turning off your cell phone and car radio when in your vehicle and just speaking and listening to God. (Make sure you keep your eyes open!)

Through those quiet times you will come to know His voice. You will come to understand how He speaks to you. In those times, as you search His Word for guidance—and then listen—you will begin to "hear" His voice. This is not some mystical, out-of-this-world event; it is simply the reality of God's Holy Spirit at work in your life.

You will hear God's voice through Christian friends, your pastor, or through certain events. You'll recognize it as you become more familiar with God's work in your life. God does not leave you to your own devices. He calls you to come to Him with your desires, your requests, your needs. Just as you would want your children to come to you with whatever is on their minds, so God wants that from you.

PRAY BECAUSE IT HELPS YOU

What a God we have who plans a way for us to communicate with Him! For Christians, prayer is a joyous part of our relationship with Him. Here are a few ways prayer helps us:

- Prayer helps us to keep our dependence upon God.

- Prayer helps us to get our perspective back—especially when we come to prayer first adoring God, then confessing our sins, then thanking Him, and finally presenting our needs to Him in supplication. (Remember ACTS?)

- Prayer helps us overcome anxiety and worry. We looked at this verse previously, but it is worth noting again: "Don't worry about anything; instead, pray about everything. Tell God what you need, and thank him for all he has done" (Philippians 4:6, NLT).

- Prayer helps us to resist Satan and his temptations. "For we are not fighting against people made of flesh and blood, but against the evil rulers and authorities of the unseen world, against those mighty powers of darkness who rule this world, and against wicked spirits in the heavenly realms….Pray at all times and on every occasion in the power of the Holy Spirit. Stay alert and be persistent in your prayers for all Christians everywhere" (Ephesians 6:12, 18, NLT).

- Prayer helps us to see the will of God more clearly.

   What a blessing God gave us when He gave us prayer!

PRAY BECAUSE IT PREPARES YOU FOR JESUS' RETURN

Prayer is one of the ways in which we make ourselves ready for Christ's return.

> Be always on the watch, and pray that you may be able to escape all that is about to happen, and that you may be able to stand before the Son of Man. (Luke 21:36, NIV)

But of that day and hour no one knows, not even the angels in heaven, nor the Son, but only the Father. Take heed, watch and pray; for you don't know when the time is. (Mark 13:32-33)

Jesus is going to come back—He promised that to us! In the meantime, we are to live for Him on this planet. His goal is to make us "mature and complete, not lacking anything" (James 1:4, NIV).

Why?

Because He is preparing us for heaven. And we want to be ready!

Perhaps one of the most poignant pictures of our need for prayer comes from C. S. Lewis. In the book *The Magician's Nephew* (one of the Chronicles of Narnia), two children are sent by Aslan (the figure of Christ in the story) to do an important task. They are transported by a flying horse named Fledge, and when they land for the night, the children are very hungry. Fledge is quite surprised at this, for he didn't know that children don't eat grass.

One of them, Digory, said, "Well, I do think someone might have arranged about our meals."

"I'm sure Aslan would have, if you'd asked him," said Fledge.

"Wouldn't he know without being asked?" said Polly.

"I've no doubt he would," said the horse (still with his mouth full). "But I've a sort of idea he likes to be asked."

Our God likes to be asked. So ask.

ELEVEN
OBSTACLES TO EFFECTIVE PRAYER

Prayer is an awesome privilege. Prayer is your lifeline to God. Prayer is your vehicle for staying close to Him and living in line with His will for you.

So guess what? *Satan doesn't like it.* In fact, he hates it. He hates the fact that you can receive guidance from God and stay on the right pathway for your life. He hates the fact that God comes to help you when you call on Him in times of difficulty and temptation. He hates your quiet time when you meditate on all God has done for you. As an old hymn of the church says, "Satan trembles when he sees the weakest saint upon his knees."

The devil's "end game" is to destroy you in any way he can. But he also recognizes that you have committed your life to Christ and are under divine protection—so his second-best plan is to *immobilize* you. And one of the best ways to do this is to stop you from praying.

In the next few pages, we will look at some of the things that can go wrong in a Christian's prayer life—not to worry you or cause you alarm, but just to make you aware of potential pitfalls you may face.

THE PROBLEM OF PRIDE

Who would think that during something as spiritual as the act of prayer we could be capable of sin? Jesus shows very clearly that this is not only possible, it can really be a problem. Even while praying we can be guilty of hypocrisy and self-centeredness—the sin of pride.

Jesus told a parable of a Pharisee (a religious leader) and a tax collector (a despised Jewish person who collected taxes for the Romans):

> Two men went to the Temple to pray. One was a Pharisee, and the other was a dishonest tax collector. The proud Pharisee stood by himself and prayed this prayer: "I thank you, God, that I am not a sinner like everyone else, especially like that tax collector over there! For I never cheat, I don't sin, I don't commit adultery, I fast twice a week, and I give you a tenth of my income." But the tax collector stood at a distance and dared not even lift his eyes to heaven as he prayed. Instead, he beat his chest in sorrow, saying, "O God, be merciful to me, for I am a sinner." I tell you, this sinner, not the Pharisee, returned home justified before God. For the proud will be humbled, but the humble will be honored. (Luke 18:10-14, NLT)

The Pharisee had the reputation of a man of God; the tax collector had the reputation of a turncoat, a traitor, and a greedy, dishonest cheat. Pharisees were admired; tax collectors were scorned. Many of them not only collected the taxes Rome required but added more to the amounts they collected and kept it for themselves (that was legal—Rome didn't care as long as it got its cut).

So here we have this Pharisee and this tax collector—almost like saying a minister and a drug dealer—going into a church to pray. You get the idea.

Now, immediately you might think that the Pharisee (or the minister) has the direct line to God. God will obviously hear and answer this holy man. But Jesus throws us a curve (as He often does!).

The problem was that the Pharisee wasn't praying to talk to God at all; he was praying to be heard and admired by those around him. He was actually bragging about his accomplishments in prayer! Jesus declared that it wasn't the Pharisee's but the tax collector's prayer that was heard—because he came in reverence to God, knowing he was a sinner who needed mercy.

Jesus spoke at other times about religious leaders who would "pray publicly on street corners and in the synagogues where everyone can see them" (Matthew 6:5). Apparently, their public prayers—maybe long-winded and self-congratulatory—made people think that they were really holy people. But because their prayers were meant more for the people to hear than for God to hear, Jesus explained that the praise of the people was "all the reward they will ever get."

OBSTACLES TO EFFECTIVE PRAYER

You will have private times of prayer with God, and you will have times of corporate prayer with other believers—either in small groups where you may pray aloud or in groups where you are simply joining with others in prayer. Both are important. But it's interesting to note when reading the Gospels that Jesus' prayers were short when offered in public and very lengthy when He was alone with God. He could spend a whole night in communion with His Father.

How different with so many believers. Many have short prayers in private but long prayers in public. Perhaps some people pray such long prayers in front of others because, like the Pharisees, they want to impress people with their devotion to God. But it doesn't impress God, and He is the one to whom prayer should be addressed.

When you want to have a heart-to-heart talk with someone, would you do it with an audience? If you would, what do you think would be your motive?

When you want to have a serious talk with a friend, you do it privately, at a time when you won't be disturbed. That's what your communication with God is like. There are times when you will pray with other believers, but those times of corporate prayer should come out of already having solid private time in prayer with God. Getting together with a group is not a substitute for private prayer.

And one more note: Besides the ones who are praying long-winded prayers to impress people, you may come across some whose "prayer requests" are just thinly veiled gossip: "Lord, you know that Jim has been cheating at school and sleeping with his girlfriend, and we ask you to show him the right way"; or "Father, you know Ed has been having financial problems lately...." You can discuss anything you want with God in private, but the words you pray publicly need to be carefully chosen.

VAIN REPETITIONS

Another problem Jesus addressed was prayers that were ritualized, repeated over and over with little attention paid to what was said. He told His followers, "Don't babble on and on as people of other religions do. They think their prayers are answered only by repeating their words again and again" (Matthew 6:7, NLT).

Using pre written prayers becomes a problem when we say them over and over as our only prayer. Why? Because if we aren't careful, we find ourselves reciting them without even thinking about what we're saying. "For this food we are about to receive..." you say; meanwhile, you're thinking about what you're going to do after dinner. What kind of praying is that?

Don't misunderstand. Written prayers aren't bad in themselves. The point is that they shouldn't be your *only* prayers. Your prayer time can be—and should be—like getting together with your very best friend to talk things over. You don't have the same conversation every time you meet!

PRAYERS THAT GO NOWHERE

Most believers have times when they feel as though their prayers are "hitting the ceiling." Although God is certainly in all places at all times and always ready to listen to His children, Scripture makes it clear that there are things that get in the way of His answering.

UNCONFESSED SIN

The prophet Isaiah explained to the people: 'Listen! The Lord is not too weak to save you, and he is not becoming deaf. He can hear you when you call. But there is a problem—your sins have cut you off from God. Because of your sin, he has turned away and won't listen anymore" (Isaiah 59:1-2, NLT).

We discussed this earlier in the book, looking at the psalmist's words, "If I had cherished sin in my heart, the Lord would not have listened" (Psalm 66:18, NIV).

Again, it's not that God expects you never to sin again. The problem arises when you know what you should do but don't do it; when you cherish sin in your heart; when you hold on to something that you know is a sin and refuse to give it up. If God is speaking to you about a sin you need to abandon, and you refuse to do so, then you can't expect that He's going to answer your prayers. In a way, you have terminated the conversation with Him.

WRONG MOTIVES

James encourages us to look at the motives behind our prayers. "When you ask, you don't receive, because you ask with wrong motives, that you may spend what you get on your pleasures" (James 4:3, NIV).

Some might pray, "God, use me!" but deep down they want God to use them so that they can become famous and have people speak their name. Their motive is not God's glory, but their own.

Or a young man might pray, "Lord, save that girl!" not because he is concerned about her spiritual state, but because he has already become romantically involved with her, knowing she isn't a believer, and he feels guilty about it.

James didn't want us to be praying carelessly. We need to examine ourselves, making sure that our selfish desires don't contaminate our prayers. What is the motive behind your request? What will you do to glorify God if the Lord answers your prayer with a yes? Do you believe that what you are praying for is truly God's will? Is what you are requesting in the best interest of God's kingdom?

IDOLS IN OUR LIVES

The prophet Ezekiel wrote,

> Son of man, these leaders have set up idols in their hearts. They have embraced things that lead them into sin. Why should I let them ask me anything? (Ezekiel 14:3, NLT)

You may be thinking, This one's not about me. I don't bow down before any idols. But what is an idol? *It is anything or anyone that takes the place of God in your life.* An idol can be any object, idea, philosophy, habit, occupation, sport, or whatever has your primary concern and loyalty. Our bodies can be idols if we spend all of our time and energy worrying about exercise or diet. If it gets in the way of our time with God ("I'll go to the gym at 5:00 A.M., but I won't have time for my prayer or Bible study"), it may have become an idol.

What about our jobs? Would we do anything to keep a certain job—even actions that would disappoint God? Do we allow our work to take over our lives to the degree that we don't have the time or energy to think about Him? Then our work is an idol.

What about our possessions? Are they so important to us that we could not give anything up if God wanted us to? Do we spend all of our time worrying about them to the point that we cannot trust in God to care for us? Or do we want certain possessions so much that we will do anything to get them? Are we so focused on the things we want that we can't think of anything else? Then our possessions (or the possessions we desire) are idols.

What about other people? Do we want them to think well of us, so we keep quiet about our faith? Are we afraid of what people might think? Perhaps some friends are dragging us down spiritually. Whenever we spend time with them, we are worse off for it. God warns us, "Don't follow the advice of the wicked" (Psalm 1:1, NLT). When we do, such people could become idols in our lives.

Until you deal with these things, your prayer life won't be what it ought to be.

LACK OF FORGIVENESS

Forgiven people should be forgiving people. An unforgiving attitude is one of the most common hindrances to prayer. Are you nursing a grudge against someone? You need to let it go. After all, when you consider all that God has forgiven you, is that too much to ask?

Jesus told a parable about this:

> "For this reason, the Kingdom of Heaven can be compared to a king who decided to bring his accounts up to date with servants who had borrowed money from him. In the process, one of his debtors was brought in who owed him millions of dollars. He couldn't pay, so the king ordered that he, his wife, his children, and everything he had be sold to pay the debt. But the man fell down before the king and begged him, 'Oh, sir, be patient with me, and I will pay it all.' Then the king was filled with pity for him, and he released him and forgave his debt.

"But when the man left the king, he went to a fellow servant who owed him a few thousand dollars. He grabbed him by the throat and demanded instant payment. His fellow servant fell down before him and begged for a little more time. 'Be patient and I will pay it,' he pleaded. But his creditor wouldn't wait. He had the man arrested and jailed until the debt could be paid in full.

"When some of the other servants saw this, they were very upset. They went to the king and told him what had happened. Then the king called in the man he had forgiven and said, 'You evil servant! I forgave you that tremendous debt because you pleaded with me. Shouldn't you have mercy on your fellow servant, just as I had mercy on you?' Then the angry king sent the man to prison until he had paid every penny.

"That's what my heavenly Father will do to you if you refuse to forgive your brothers and sisters in your heart." (Matthew 18:23-35, NLT)

God's forgiveness is unlimited; therefore, our forgiveness should be as well. When we don't forgive others, we are showing that we don't understand or appreciate the forgiveness that God has given us. And it hinders our ability to pray.

God desires to communicate with you, but have you "hung up" on Him? If so, it's time to redial His number. First you must deal with the areas addressed in this chapter. Check your motives, confess your sins, make sure there are no idols in your life, and forgive those who have hurt you.

Listen to what God says to us: "Call to me and I will answer you and tell you great and unsearchable things you don't know" (Jeremiah 33:3, NIV).

TWELVE
PRAYER THAT PREVAILS

I n this final chapter we're going to unlock some of the secrets of
prayer that make use of its power and potential.
Let's look at the book of Acts where we see the power of prayer in action.

> After the apostles Peter and John had been threatened
> by the Jewish leaders to stop preaching about Jesus, they
> "found the other believers and told them what the leading
> priests and elders had said. Then all the believers were
> united as they lifted their voices in prayer… (Acts 4:23-24, NLT).

The early believers faced intense persecution. The Jewish leaders
sought to keep them quiet. They seized Peter and John and put them in
jail at one point, and at another time, they imprisoned all the apostles.

Things came to a head when they actually stoned Stephen for

proclaiming Jesus as Lord. Acts 12 tells the story of a time when King Herod arrested some of the believers. The king wanted to "stay in good" with the Jewish leaders in Jerusalem, so he had James executed. (This was James, the brother of John, and one of Jesus' earliest disciples.) Being the consummate politician, Herod, when he "saw how much this pleased the Jewish leaders...arrested Peter during the Passover celebration" (Acts 12:3).

When the Jewish leaders had imprisoned the apostles previously, they miraculously escaped, so this time Herod took extra precautions. Peter was under the guard of four squads of four soldiers each—that's sixteen men guarding him! Herod wanted to bring Peter out for public trial after the Passover—hoping, surely, to have the same result that had been accomplished with a previous prisoner named Jesus.

He had executed James; Peter was next.

So Peter was in prison, and what did the church do? Boycott all products made in Rome as a protest? Gather with swords to go down and try to take on the Roman soldiers guarding him? No, the church used its "secret weapon." The Bible tells us that "constant prayer was offered to God for him by the church" (Acts 12:5).

All other doors may have been closed, but one remained open—the door of prayer. The way to secure release for Peter was through God by means of prayer.

So often prayer is our last resort when it should be our first! Let's see what Scripture says about the prayers of these early followers of Jesus.

PREVAILING PRAYER IS OFFERED TO GOD

Acts 12:5 says that prayer was "offered to God."

"Well, of course," you might say. "Isn't all prayer offered to God?" No, actually, it isn't. Often when we pray, our minds are so taken up with the thought of what we need that there is very little thought of God Himself. For prayer to be powerful and effective, there needs to be a recognition of the One to whom we are speaking.

Earlier, we observed that the model prayer Jesus taught His followers began, "Our Father in heaven, hallowed be your name…." In other words, prevailing prayer begins with the concept of going into the presence of God, your Father in heaven, who is perfect, holy, and awesome.

Needless to say, if you are in a life-threatening situation, a hearty "HELP!" will suffice. But under normal circumstances, we need to slow down and contemplate just who this awesome God is that we are praying to. Prayer should never be taken for granted. It is a privilege. So when you come into God's presence, come with reverence and awe, deeply grateful that He invites you there, that He listens, and that He will answer.

PREVAILING PRAYER IS PASSIONATE

Acts 12:5 in the New King James Version says that the believers' prayers were "constant." Other versions say that they prayed "earnestly."

These believers weren't casual or flippant about their prayers on Peter's behalf. They didn't say, "Dear Lord, (yawn), please save Peter…or whatever (zzzzzz)…."

No, these prayers were literally storming the gates of heaven. You can almost hear them praying with tears and in agony, worried that Peter would soon face the same fate that their dear friend James had just experienced. These people prayed passionately, "Dear Lord, DELIVER PETER!!!"

The word passionate speaks of a soul that is filled with intense desire. The same word is used of Jesus in Luke 22:44 (NIV), "He prayed more earnestly, and his sweat was like drops of blood falling to the ground."

Prayer that prevails with God is prayer into which we put our whole soul, stretching out toward Him in intense and agonizing desire. Many of our prayers have no power in them because there is no heart in them! If we put so little heart into our prayers, we cannot expect God to put much heart into answering them. God promises that His people will find Him when they search for Him with all their heart.

PREVAILING PRAYER IS PERSISTENT

Prayer that prevails is persistent. This "constant" prayer of the believers probably continued through several days and nights. Peter wasn't released until the night before the planned trial, but the believers kept on praying—and they were still praying when Peter arrived on their doorstep!

Remember the story Jesus told of the woman who needed justice from the corrupt judge? The point of the parable is not that God is corrupt and we have to nag Him for answers to our prayers: "Lord, you better come through on this or you'll have me to deal with!"

Yet some people pray that way. They feel they have to convince God because He really doesn't care. Or they feel they have to pray louder or longer to get Him to pay attention.

To be blunt, those are *pagan* concepts.

That's like the prophets of the false god Baal in the Old Testament calling loudly to him for hours on end. They ended up rolling around on the ground and slashing themselves with knives to try to get their god's attention (see 1 Kings 18).

No, our God is not like the corrupt judge. And no, He is not a silent and lifeless idol. Our God is the exact opposite. In fact, Jesus ends that parable by explaining that if even a corrupt judge will end up giving justice when someone is persistent, how much more will God's children receive what is right from their loving heavenly Father! "So don't be afraid, little flock. For it gives your Father great happiness to give you the Kingdom" (Luke 12:32, NLT).

We don't have to threaten God or wear Him out.

We're not trying to overcome His reluctance; we are trying to take hold of His willingness. We're not trying to bend God our way, but seeking to bend His way. We're not trying to get our will into heaven but to get His will on earth.

PREVAILING PRAYER IS PRAYED WITH FAITH

Clearly there is an important place for faith in our prayers. And, no doubt, there are many occasions where God's work has been hindered because of unbelief. Having stated that, it is important for us to realize that it won't always be our faith that brings answers; sometimes it will be the faith of others.

Mark 5 tells us the story of a woman who had been having a problem with bleeding for twelve years. She had been to many doctors, and no one had been able to heal her disease. But "she had heard about Jesus, so she came up behind him through the crowd and touched the fringe of his robe. For she thought to herself, 'If I can just touch his clothing, I will be healed.' Immediately the bleeding stopped, and she could feel that she had been healed!" (Mark 5:27-29, NLT).

Jesus noticed that someone had touched Him, for He "realized at once that healing power had gone out from him" (Mark 5:30, NLT), and He sought out the person who had touched Him for healing. When the woman admitted it, Jesus kindly said to her, "Daughter, your faith has made you well. Go in peace. You have been healed" (Mark 5:34, NLT).

In this woman's case, Jesus responded to her faith.

Matthew 8:5-13 tells us the story of a Roman centurion (a commander or officer in the Roman army). He came to Jesus to request healing for his servant. Jesus said that He would come, but the Roman commander said, "Lord, I am not worthy to have you come into my home. Just say the word from where you are, and my servant will be healed!" (v. 8, NLT).

Jesus was astounded at such faith and answered, "What you have believed has happened" (v. 13, NLT). In this man's case, it was his faith that Jesus honored, not the faith of the one who needed the healing touch.

Finally, there is the story of Lazarus in John 11. Lazarus was a friend of Jesus. When he died, Jesus went to raise him from the dead. But Lazarus could have no faith on his own behalf; he was dead. His sisters, Mary and Martha, had believed that Jesus could heal Lazarus, but once he was dead, their hope was gone. The religious leaders who came to comfort Mary and Martha wondered why Jesus had not come back sooner.

There was so much doubt that day that Jesus wept. But God intervened mightily and raised Lazarus from the dead. In the case of Lazarus, it wasn't the faith of the one being touched or the faith of another on his or her behalf; it was simply God intervening despite the imperfect faith of His people.

And that's what God did for this group of believers. As you will see by the end of the story, they didn't really believe God would intervene as mightily as He did! But God can use our imperfect prayers to do His perfect will.

PRAYER POWER

So what happened with that passionate, persistent prayer offered to God on Peter's behalf? Let's look at the rest of the story, recorded in Acts 12:6-19.

Peter was jailed but not worried. In fact, the night before the trial, Peter was chained between two soldiers—and he was asleep! Talk about calm in the midst of the storm! He was probably the only believer in town asleep that night. The rest were praying.

Suddenly an angel appeared in the cell, woke Peter up (had to strike him, actually, because he was so sound asleep), and told him to get up and get dressed. Immediately, the chains fell from Peter's wrists. The angel told Peter to follow, and he did. Peter thought he was seeing a vision as he was led out of the prison, past the first and second sets of guards, and through an iron gate that opened by itself to let him through. Then he walked to the end of the block, and the angel left him.

Peter suddenly realized that this was indeed real, so he went to the home of Mary, mother of John (Mark), where people were gathered together praying for him.

He knocked on the door, and a girl named Rhoda came to answer it. She heard Peter's voice and ran back into the house to tell everyone that the beloved apostle was at the door.

In the meantime she left poor old Peter standing outside in the cold! The believers looked up from their fervent prayers for Peter's deliverance and basically said, "Right, Rhoda. Nice try. You're crazy."

But the very answer to their prayer was outside knocking. Finally someone else got up and went to the door and discovered—PETER!

Look at how God changed the situation in Acts 12 as a result of prayer. In the beginning of the chapter, a seemingly all-powerful King Herod was wreaking havoc on the Christians in Jerusalem. He had on his side the power of Rome. He executed one of their own and imprisoned another. The situation appeared hopeless.

The believers, however, had the power of God on their side—and their secret weapon: prayer.

The chapter ends with the great King Herod giving a speech met with such adulation that the people called him a god. Herod absorbed the praise as if he deserved it, and God dealt with him so severely that he died a horrible death.

The chapter opens with Peter in prison and Herod triumphing; it closes with Herod dead, Peter free, and God triumphing.

A FINAL WORD

I hope that, having heard all these stories of answered prayer, you are saying, "I want to learn how to pray to a God that powerful!"

Because you can.

You are a child of God, so you have the awesome privilege of prayer.

Please understand that *you don't have to be perfect to pray*. Listen to one more encouraging story, found in Mark 9:14-29 (NLT). A man brought his demon-possessed son to Jesus, asking Jesus to cast out the demon. "The evil spirit often makes him fall into the fire or into water, trying to kill him. Have mercy on us and help us. Do something if you can," he said (v. 22).

To which Jesus responded, "What do you mean, 'If I can'?....

Anything is possible if a person believes" (v. 23).

The father understood but truthfully acknowledged his greatest fear. He tearfully said to Jesus, "Lord, I believe; help my unbelief!" (Mark 9:24). Did Jesus respond, "Well, I'm sorry; that's just not enough"? No. Jesus answered the man's prayer and healed his son.

Pray with passion, persistence, and as much faith as you can muster. God knows you are an imperfect person. Just say to Him, "Lord, I believe; help my unbelief!"

And you know what? He'll answer that prayer, too!

PART THREE
SHARING
THE
GOOD NEWS

THIRTEEN
THE BURDEN

I was as green as they come, as far as sharing the gospel went. Yet there I was, a young teenager out on the beach, looking for someone to talk to about my newfound faith in Christ. It didn't turn out the way I had expected.

I was only two weeks old in my commitment to Christ. I didn't know much about Christian living or the Bible, but I had heard that I should go out and share the gospel with others. So one day I went down to the beach—the same beach where I used to make a point of avoiding any Bible-toting Christians who might try convert me.

Now here I was—a bona fide member of the "Soul Patrol"—out prowling for unbelievers to convert. But I wasn't exactly full of confidence. In fact, my main goal was to find someone who wouldn't argue or get angry at me. I thought if an unbeliever just ignored me or walked away, that would be fine.

Eventually, I spotted a middle-aged lady who looked about the age of my mom. I figured she might be somewhat sympathetic to me. When I walked up to her, my voice trembled with nervousness. "Uh, excuse me," I said, fumbling for the right words. "Can I talk to you about something?"

She said, "Sure. What about?"

"Well, about, like, God—and stuff," I answered. (Remember, I was still a teenager.)

To my amazement, she said, "Go ahead. Sit down. Talk to me."

I then pulled out a copy of an evangelistic tract I had stuffed in my pocket for a moment like this. I was so new in the faith that I hadn't even memorized the plan of salvation, so I just read through the entire booklet verbatim. The whole time I read, I was shaking like a leaf and thinking, *This isn't going to work. Why am I doing this? This is not going to reach her.* But the woman continued to patiently listen to what I was saying—rather, reading.

When I got to a part in the booklet that said, "Is there any good reason why you should not accept Jesus Christ right now?" I realized that I should direct this question to the woman. I hesitated. Feeling awkward, I looked up and asked her, "Uh, is there any good reason why you should not accept Jesus Christ right now?"

"No," she replied.

"Okay," I said, slightly confused. "Then that would mean that you do want to accept Jesus Christ right now?"

With a look of quiet resolve, she answered, "Yes, I would."

I was shocked. For a moment I didn't know what to do. I had only planned for failure. Frantically I searched the tract for some kind of prayer in which to lead a person who wanted to invite Christ into his or her life. After what seemed an eternity, I finally found one. In the most reverent tone I could muster, I said, "Let's bow our heads for a word of prayer."

Even as she prayed after me, I was still thinking, *This is not going to work.* After we were done, the woman looked up at me and said,

"Something just happened to me!"

And at that moment something happened to me, too: I got a taste of what it was like to be used by God. I knew—even at that point at that young age—that no matter what I did in life, I wanted to continue to share the gospel.

BURDENED FOR UNBELIEVERS

Any effective sharing of one's faith will always begin with a God-given burden for lost people—those who don't know Christ. And if some of us today were brutally honest, we would have to say that we don't have that burden. If we did, quite frankly, I think many of us would do more than we do.

"But I'm not qualified or an expert on theology," some might protest. Let me put it this way: Let's say that you are walking down the street and hear the screams of a woman. You turn to see what the problem is, and she points to a burning house and hysterically cries that her little baby is inside. You realize that you have only moments before the entire house will be engulfed with flames.

Would you simply walk away, reasoning that it was her child and not yours? Not likely. Would you try to quiet her down and tell her to wait until the professionals arrive? Possibly, but again, not likely. Would you risk your own life and try to get into that building and save that child? I would hope so.

A fate even worse than that awaits those who do not know Christ. For them, the fire is not temporary but eternal. Do we honestly care? People can tell if we really do when we talk to them about our faith in Christ. They can sense if we are simply doing it out of duty and our heart is not really in it.

I have seen Christians share the gospel in an almost mechanical way. They have their canned statements and answers. They aren't really engaged. This will ultimately defeat their own purpose.

You can talk about love all you want. You can cite the various

Greek words the Bible uses to describe it. You can even quote numerous passages from Scripture to prove the importance of it. But the best thing you can do is to demonstrate it as you share your faith. To do that effectively, you need a God-given burden.

BURDENED TO GET INVOLVED

We need to have a burden like Jesus had for the people of Jerusalem. Scripture describes his heartfelt burden as he looked out over Jerusalem one day and wept, saying, "O Jerusalem, Jerusalem, the one who kills the prophets and stones those who are sent to her! How often I wanted to gather your children together, as a hen gathers her chicks under her wings, but you were not willing!" (Matthew 23:37).

The apostle Paul echoes that sentiment in Romans 9:2-3: "I have great sorrow and continual grief in my heart. For I could wish that I myself were accursed from Christ for my brethren, my countrymen according to the flesh."

No wonder Paul had such a powerful and effective ministry. He cared!

Nehemiah is another classic illustration of a man who was genuinely touched with the needs of the lost. As cupbearer to the king of Persia, he was in a position of great power and influence. While possessing this status and prestige, he was also a Jew—one of the many who had been in exile away from Jerusalem. Nehemiah could have easily kicked back and set up house on easy street.

One day his brother came back from a visit to Jerusalem and told Nehemiah about the destruction he had seen. The once proud and erect walls of the city were now simply heaps of charred rubble. Nehemiah recognized that these walls were a symbol of a people who once stood with God, separated from the pagan nations around them. But now they lay in ruin.

This revelation so broke Nehemiah's heart that he wept. Yet after Nehemiah's weeping came working. After his despair came determination. He could have rationalized his way out of personally doing anything by saying, "I'm no priest or prophet. Let them take care of it! Besides, if I speak up, I may jeopardize my coveted position with the king. And what good would *that* do?"

But Nehemiah realized that he, a layman, could make a difference. So he prayed, and he obtained permission from the king to go and personally assess the damage. After Nehemiah did that, he drafted a plan and acted upon it (Nehemiah 1–2).

It's not enough to only plan. It's not even enough to only pray. We have to move when God tells us to move. When Moses was on the shore of the Red Sea with the Egyptian army in hot pursuit, the Lord said to Moses, "Why are you crying out to me? Tell the people to get moving!" (Exodus 14:15, NLT).

There is a time to pray and a time to move—a time to sow and a time to reap. But it all starts with a God-given burden for lost people. Alexander McClaren said, "You tell me the depth of a Christian's compassion, and I will tell you the measure of his usefulness." To quote the great British pastor C. H. Spurgeon, "Winners of souls must first be weepers of souls." This is essential to effectively sharing your faith.

GRIPPED WITH URGENCY

I would suggest the reason many Christians have never led another person to Christ is that we have never really asked a person that pivotal question: "Would you like to accept Jesus Christ into your life as your personal Savior?"

Instead, we chicken out at the last minute.

What if they say no? we may wonder. Our real fear might actually be, *What if they say yes?*

If they do say yes—and I believe that if you are actively sharing your faith, you will eventually get such an answer—it will be one of the greatest joys you will ever know this side of heaven. Just think— a person's eternal destiny has changed! A person who had been on his way to hell is now going to heaven. A person who was empty and lonely is now fulfilled and complete—all because you took the time to share the gospel message.

Even so, too many of us give up too easily. We may ask our unbelieving friends, "Do you want to come to church with me?"

"No," they flatly reply.

"Okay, never mind," you say, dropping the subject (and perhaps feeling slightly relieved).

How can we give up so easily? Do we really believe what we claim to believe? Are we convinced of the reality of a heaven and a hell? Do we actually accept that the wages of sin really are death? If so, how can we be so casual about telling others?

Many years ago in England, a criminal named Charles Peace was arrested. He was a burglar, a forger, and he was guilty of double murder. He was condemned to death for his crimes. As he was making his way to the gallows on the day of his execution, a chaplain walked by his side. This minister was simply "going through the motions," speaking coldly of the importance of faith and belief. In the course of his oft-repeated speech, the minister mentioned the power of Jesus Christ to save from sin.

Suddenly the criminal spun around, looked the chaplain in the eye, and exclaimed, "Do you believe that? Do you really believe that? If I believed that, I would willingly crawl across England on broken glass to tell men it was true."

If we really believe what we are sharing, we should be gripped with the urgency of the message. I want to encourage you and help you to see that God can indeed use you to bring others into his kingdom.

SHARING, NOT CONVERTING

Without question, conversion is the work of the Holy Spirit. Jesus says, "No one can come to me unless the Father who sent Me draws him" (John 6:44, NIV).

Paul also reminds us, "Neither he who plants nor he who waters is anything, but only God, who makes things grow. The man who plants and the man who waters have one purpose, and each will be rewarded according to his own labor" (1 Corinthians 3:7-8, NIV).

There is nothing you or I can do to make a person convert. I've heard Billy Graham tell the story of a very inebriated man who happened to be on the same flight as the famed evangelist. Hearing Billy was on board, this drunken man demanded to speak with him. The flight attendants tried to keep the man in his seat, but he would not be satisfied until he had spoken with Billy himself.

Hearing about this, Billy got out of his seat and greeted the man.

The drunken man said, "Billy, I'm glad to meet you! I'm one of your converts!"

Billy thought to himself, *He must be one of my converts. He certainly isn't one of the Lord's!*

Only God can bring about a true conversion.

Sometimes we get to a certain place in our gospel presentation where we may feel compelled to apply a little pressure. We want to close the deal—possibly before it's ready to happen. Remember, our job is to clearly and accurately present the gospel message, leaving the results to God. As Sergeant Friday of the classic TV program Dragnet used to say, "Just the facts, ma'am."

Of course, you must be ready to "pull in the net" if the person is ready. If that individual is not at that point, however, leave the timing to God.

Statistics tell us that 95 percent of all Christians have never led another person to Christ. Are you in that massive percentage? Or are you in that "elite few" who have had the privilege of helping a person pass from darkness to light?

I believe that God can and will use you to lead others to himself. I don't think that bringing others to Christ is only the work of a select few. Granted, some have been specifically called to be evangelists. That is a gift that comes from God, and it is not limited to those who may hold evangelistic crusades (though it obviously includes them).

It is a calling that I have personally seen in the lives of those who are in their seventies as well as those who are still very young.

These individuals simply have a special way of freely sharing the gospel with astounding results. But don't let that discourage you. For although biblical principles will enable you to more effectively tell others about Jesus Christ, you must first understand that there is both a right and wrong way to share the gospel. Second, you will learn that certain essentials need to be in place for the gospel to be the gospel.

FOURTEEN
ARE WE THE OBSTACLE?

I t's been said that there are two reasons people don't go to church:
(1) They don't know a Christian, or (2) they do.

Sometimes in our inexperience or overzealous ways, we are our
own worst enemies. We console ourselves with the verse that says,
"Blessed are those who are persecuted for righteousness' sake" (Matthew 5:10), when in reality we are sometimes "persecuted" for being
obnoxious, strange, or just plain weird!

Many times, unbelievers are not rejecting the gospel itself as much
as they are rejecting the way it is presented. They don't necessarily
object to what is inside the box; they just don't like its wrapping.

That is not to say that there is no offense in the message of the gospel.
Indeed, it can and will be offensive at times. Acknowledging a holy God
and a place of eternal judgment will bother and even offend some people.

Yet at the same time, let's make sure it is the gospel they are offended by instead of some bizarre thing an alleged follower of Christ says or does.

I must admit that it really is a mystery that God has chosen to use people as the primary communicators of his truth in the first place—and that he has chosen preaching as His primary method of communication! Romans 10:14-15 (NLT) says, "How can they call on him to save them unless they believe in him? And how can they believe in him if they have never heard about him? And how can they hear about him unless someone tells them? And how will anyone go and tell them without being sent? That is what the Scriptures mean when they say, 'How beautiful are the feet of those who bring good news!'"

The apostle Paul reiterates this message in 1 Corinthians 1:21:

> Since, in the wisdom of God, the world through wisdom didn't know God, it pleased God through the foolishness of the message preached to save those who believe."

That verse doesn't say that God uses foolish preaching (of which there is plenty, unfortunately) to save those who believe; nor does it say that preaching a "foolish" message (though it will be perceived as such to some) will effectively do the work. For again Scripture reminds us, "The message of the cross is foolishness to those who are perishing" (1 Corinthians 1:18).

Paul is essentially pointing out how simple, unexpected, and unbelievable it is that through basic verbal communication (backed by the power of the Spirit and a godly life), a person's eternal destiny can be instantaneously changed!

It seems to me that it would be much more effective for God to roll away the heavens, poke his head through the clouds and say, "Hello, humanity! I'm God, and you are not. So I strongly suggest that you all believe in Me right now."

Somehow I think that would get a good response. Or He could send thousands of angels in all of their splendor to proclaim the gospel. But He has not chosen to work that way. Instead, He has primarily chosen to use people like you and me.

A LESSON FROM THE TITANIC

Through the help of Hollywood and the passing of time, we have all come to know the story of the sinking of the Titanic. One of the things that makes this tragedy so captivating is the realization that the story could have been different had the ship's captain and crew not made so many disastrous decisions and mistakes.

We've learned how those in charge repeatedly and flagrantly ignored the warnings of ice ahead. We know that the captain tried to steer the ship around the fatal iceberg instead of hitting it head-on, which, with the advantage of hindsight, would have been the better choice.

We also know that there weren't enough lifeboats on board. One of the greatest tragedies of the Titanic story is that when the massive ship went under, many of those lifeboats were only half full! Those in the lifeboats could hear the screams of the people (many of them their husbands and sons), yet not one boat went back until one long hour had passed.

They returned after the screams had subsided. They rowed back to the people only when they felt it was safe. But it was too late.

Listen! The screams of those who are without Christ can be heard. They may not even realize the severity of their situation yet, but they cry out to us. We must go and pull them into the lifeboat!

To quote the wise C. H. Spurgeon again, this is what we must remember when we bring the gospel to those who don't yet know him:

> The Holy Spirit will move them by first moving you. If you can rest without their being saved, they will rest, too. But if you are filled with an agony for them, if you cannot bear that they should be lost, you will soon find that they are uneasy, too. I hope you will get into such a state that you will dream about your child or your hearer perishing for lack of Christ, and start up at once and begin to cry, "Oh God, give me converts or I will die." Then you will have converts.

DISTORTIONS OF THE MESSAGE

Some years ago, I was walking down the main street of Waikiki in Hawaii. I saw a man standing on one of the corners with a rather large sign. Emblazoned on the sign were the words The Wages of Sin Is Death! It also had some flames painted on it, no doubt for effect.

Yelling at the top of his voice to every passerby, the overly zealous street preacher shouted such things as, "You're gonna burn!" "God will judge you, sinner!" and "Repent or perish!"

The things he was saying certainly had a ring of truth to them. At the same time, there was no love or compassion in his delivery. In fact, it almost seemed as though he took some kind of perverse pleasure in yelling this out to people. So I walked up to him and tried to get his attention.

"Excuse me—"

He continued screaming at the people passing by, "Repent, ye sinners!"

"Pardon me."

He continued yelling. Finally I got his attention.

"What do you want?" he barked.

"Well," I said, "I'm a Christian, too, but I was thinking that you are really only giving half of the gospel message out here tonight. It is true that the wages of sin is death, but I'm sure you're aware of the fact that the rest of that very verse says, 'But the gift of God is eternal life through Jesus Christ our Lord.' Why don't you put that message on the other side of your sign and turn it around every now and then so people get the whole picture?"

Then he screamed at me and told me that I was going to hell, too! It's sad when people misrepresent God like that.

Does your heart ache to share the hope of the gospel with those around you? Do you have a burden for those who don't yet know the Lord? Do you want to be a part of the solution, and not part of the problem? You might pause right now and pray something like this:

Lord, from this moment forward, I pray that You will give me a burden and concern for people who don't yet know You. Help me to see them as You do. Help me to care enough to share Your gospel with them. Give me that burden for the lost like You and the apostle Paul and Nehemiah had. Lord, I admit that at times I am afraid to step out. Please give me a new boldness to do that. I thank you in advance, Lord. In Jesus' name I pray, amen.

If you pray a prayer like that and mean it, you may never be the same again—and, I dare say, this world in which we live may not be either.

FIFTEEN
PATIENCE...AND MORE PATIENCE

Sharing the gospel is a lot like going fishing. In fact, Jesus used that very metaphor. Matthew's Gospel tells us that Jesus was walking by the Sea of Galilee when he "saw two brothers, Simon called Peter, and Andrew his brother, casting a net into the sea; for they were fishermen. He said to them, 'Follow Me, and I will make you fishers of men'" (Matthew 4:18-19).

Jesus has called all of us to "go fishing for men," too! A more literal translation of that phrase would be "I will make you catch men alive." The actual Greek verb used for catch is unique, and it occurs in only one other place in the Bible. In that instance, Paul tells us to be patient with those who oppose the truth, "that they may come to their senses and escape the snare of the devil, having been taken captive [caught alive] by him to do his will" (2 Timothy 2:26).

Here Scripture presents a striking contrast. *Either the devil will catch men alive, or we will.* So, are you ready to go fishing? Let's consider a few traits that make for a good fisherman.

LEARN TO WAIT

It takes time to catch fish. You must learn to wait—and wait and wait! Some years ago I had the opportunity to go fishing for king salmon on the Kenai River in Alaska. I was told that it took an average of fifty hours to pull one of these bad boys in, so I was prepared for a long wait. I got a few pulls on my line, then all of a sudden, Wham! That line got a tug so hard you would have thought that I had a great white shark on the end of it!

Okay, so I exaggerate. Would you believe a sixty-five-pound king salmon? For that is exactly what it was.

I reeled in as rapidly as I could, pulling so hard on my pole that it bent over almost parallel with itself. I thought it would snap at any moment. The rod held, though it quickly stripped, and I was just pulling for dear life to get this giant beast of a fish on board. I got him right to the edge of our boat, and he poked his massive head out of the water. We could not believe his size! Our guide put his net into the water and almost had him when that monster king salmon just snapped the line like a piece of thread.

That was it. I was really disappointed. But I'll tell you this much— I was ready to fish some more, encouraged by this close encounter.

KEEP FISHING

That's how sharing the gospel is. Some days you may get a big bite and almost "reel one in"! Other days you may not get anything close to a bite. So you just keep casting out your line and reeling it in. And you do it again and again.

To borrow another analogy concerning evangelism, there is

"a time to sow and a time to reap." Paul explains the process very clearly in 1 Corinthians 3:6-8 (NIV): "I planted the seed, Apollos watered it, but God made it grow. So neither he who plants nor he who waters is anything, but only God, who makes things grow. The man who plants and the man who waters have one purpose, and each will be rewarded according to his own labor."

In the book of Ecclesiastes, we read, "He has made everything beautiful in its time" (Ecclesiastes 3:11). We also find, "The end of a thing is better than its beginning; the patient in spirit is better than the proud in spirit" (Ecclesiastes 7:8, NIV).

BE PATIENT

Patient?

I don't know about you, but by nature, I am not a patient person. If I am driving on the freeway and one lane is moving slightly faster than another, I'm the guy weaving in and out of the lanes, wanting to get wherever I'm going just a little bit faster. When I go to the supermarket, I will carefully survey which line is the longest before I commit. And when I get in that "ten items or less" aisle, am I the only person who actually counts the items in the other people's carts to see if they fall within in the allotted amount?

"Excuse me, but this man has eleven items! Please stop him now!"

When I go to pick up pizza and bring it home for my family, I can't resist the temptation to have at least two pieces before I arrive at our house. And I can tell you that I have scorched the roof of my mouth more than once with the burning cheese of a pizza that needed to cool down first.

For that reason, when God tells me that I need to be patient when it comes to sharing my faith, it is not an easy task. Just as a fisherman often must sit quietly in his boat for hours at a time patiently awaiting a bite, so we "fishermen of souls" must be patient. We may not catch anything on a particular day, but we go back again, and we are patient with those to whom we share.

It is important to remember that the "final answer" may not come at the end of a church service or a conversation with someone. We have heard so many stories over the years of those who have attended our Harvest Crusades and didn't commit their lives to Christ at the actual crusade but came to the Lord later.

Sometimes it is no later than when they step out into the stadium parking lot after the meeting. At other times it may be a day, a week, or a few months or even years later.

Fishermen are patient, and so are farmers. Consider a farmer planting his field. Seed is sown, but it germinates at different times. So when we share the gospel message with others. The "seed" was sown—but it doesn't always germinate in some people as quickly as it does in others. Sometimes a seed sown today may not break ground until later.

I remember hearing one story of a father and son who were out in downtown Waikiki handing out evangelistic flyers for our Harvest Crusade. The little boy asked his dad if he could give one of the flyers to a rather burly, menacing-looking, tattooed, body-pierced man. The dad somewhat reluctantly agreed, keeping a close watch on his son.

The little boy cautiously approached this big, muscular fellow and timidly gave him the flyer. This big guy promptly snatched the flier and sort of wadded it up in his hand. From all appearances, it seemed to have been a rather unsuccessful encounter. But things aren't always as they seem.

That evening when the invitation to come to Christ was given at the crusade, that little boy and his father were waiting on the field as counselors to welcome those coming forward. One of the first was that burly guy from Waikiki, coming to receive Christ!

Sometimes the seeds we sow today may not break ground for months, years, even decades. I have preached at many funeral services where people who had been witnessed to previously by the deceased finally made a decision to follow Christ. Some of these people had heard the gospel message for years—but it wasn't until the person who had shared with them had gone on to be with the Lord that they were ready to commit their lives to Jesus.

So be patient. Be willing to wait. You may have such a burden for the lost that this is extremely difficult. But trust God, cast your line, and then be patient. After all, God needs to hook the fish!

SIXTEEN
KNOWING WHEN TO CAST

A good fisherman instinctively knows where and when to cast his line or drop his nets. The same is true of sharing our faith. We must be sensitive to the timing and leading of the Holy Spirit. As Scripture reminds us, we must "be ready in season and out of season" (2 Timothy 4:2). This could also be translated, "Be on duty at all times." We need to be ready when it comes to telling others about the Lord.

I read the story of a fisherman named Larry Shaw, who was testing an outboard propeller on a lake in Ohio a few years ago. There, in a cove, he spotted a gigantic muskellunge fish near the surface. Shaw motored toward it and unsuccessfully cast out his line several times before the fish disappeared.

A half hour later, Shaw returned to the cove where he had first spotted the big muskie. It was back! Shaw turned on the electric trolling motor and headed toward the beast. As he crept closer, the massive fish suddenly started swimming toward the boat. Shaw quickly put on a leather glove and plunged his arm into the water, grabbing the fish behind the gills. That old fish started thrashing and twisting.

Shaw was having trouble lifting the huge muskie into the boat. Fortunately, a nearby fisherman came over to help, and they were able to wrestle the monster into Shaw's boat. The muskellunge weighed over fifty-three pounds! If he had used a rod and reel, it probably would have broken the record for the biggest muskie ever caught in Ohio.

When asked about his fish, Shaw said, "I was at the right place at the right time, and I was fool enough to grab it."

That's the same attitude we should have in fishing for men. Being at the right place at the right time—and being "fool enough" to take a risk—to share the gospel.

In the book of Acts, we read the story of Philip, who was having a successful ministry of sharing the gospel down in Samaria when he was instructed by God to go to the desert (see Acts 8:26-38).

There was no detailed blueprint. No mention of whom to look for and share with. Just a command to go. But when he arrived, he found the "big fish" that Jesus had waiting for him: the treasurer for the queen of Ethiopia—a man of great importance and wealth.

In spite of his prestigious position, this man was empty and searching for the meaning of life. His search led him to Jerusalem, the spiritual capital of the world. Tragically, instead of finding the vibrant faith of days gone by, he found a cold, legalistic, dead religion that didn't give him what he needed. But he did acquire one very valuable thing from his trip there: a copy of Isaiah's writing, which would have been in scroll form.

As Philip came alongside this man's chariot, he found the man reading aloud from this scroll. Talk about a divine setup! Because Philip was ready and willing, he had the opportunity to lead that man to Christ.

TRUST GOD'S TIMING

Missionary George Smith may have thought his ministry was a failure. He had been in Africa only a short time when he was driven from the country, leaving behind only one convert: a poor woman. He died not long after that, while on his knees, praying for Africa.

Years later, a group of men stumbled onto the place where George Smith had prayed. They also found a copy of the Scriptures he had left behind in Africa. Then they met the one convert of Smith's ministry. She shared the gospel with them, and they believed. The result of their encounter with the Bible and Smith's one convert was far-reaching. One hundred years later, a mission agency discovered that more than thirteen thousand converts had emerged from the ministry that George Smith had originally begun.

Actually, the analogy of a seed taking root fits George Smith's story better than catching a fish. You obviously know when you have caught a fish, but there may be a seed of the gospel being shared that you have forgotten all about. Then one day that seed, much to the surprise of many, breaks ground. So, like missionary George Smith, we need to keep faithfully sowing the seed of the gospel—because it's not over till God has finished working.

So you fish, you plant seeds, and you trust God to work. As you are sensitive to God's leading, He'll put you in the right place at the right time. As with Philip, He'll send you to the person who needs you. As with George Smith, you may not understand the timing or see the results, but you will have accomplished God's will. And that's really what it's all about!

BUILDING THE SKILLS
KNOW GOD'S WORD

It's important that a good fisherman have the right technique. A fisherman knows his equipment: lures, hooks, floats, weights, poles, bait, etc. Likewise, as we "fish" for men and women in this sea of life, we must use the appropriate tools: the Word of God and the leading of the Spirit.

This is why we must commit portions of Scripture to memory. Returning to Philip, as that high-ranking official from Ethiopia was reading aloud from the Scriptures, he asked Philip, "Of whom does the prophet say this, of himself or of some other man?" (Acts 8:34).

Philip, the seasoned "fisher of men," knew his tools (in this case, God's Word), and he was able to pull out the right hook and reel that big fish in! He didn't falter in his reply. He knew his tools and used them well.

The use of Scripture is so important for so many reasons. For one, God promises that it won't return to him void:

> "The rain and snow come down from the heavens and stay on the ground to water the earth. They cause the grain to grow, producing seed for the farmer and bread for the hungry. It is the same with my word. I send it out, and it always produces fruit. It will accomplish all I want it to, and it will prosper everywhere I send it" (Isaiah 55:10-11, NLT).

You see, my word *will* return void.

So will yours.

But God's Word never will!

That being said, let me add a couple of important thoughts here so that we can understand the balance. While it is essential to quote Scripture, that does not mean it has to be only in King James English (which often needs to be updated to be understood in our culture). Nor do you have to get a glazed look on your face as you quote it—or yell when you quote it. (These are all things I have seen well-meaning, but ineffective, Christians do.) Nor do you have to carry a fifteen-pound family Bible. You can quote the Bible conversationally, lovingly, and in a friendly manner. This is why it is so helpful to commit large portions of Scripture to memory.

While it is good to have a copy of the Word in your briefcase or your purse, the best place to carry the Word of God is in your heart! The psalmist writes, "Your word I have hidden in my heart, that I might not sin against You" (Psalm 119:11).

Paul reminds us of the importance of doing this carefully and accurately. Instructing young Timothy, Paul says, "Be diligent to present yourself approved to God, a worker who does not need to be ashamed, rightly dividing the word of truth" (2 Timothy 2:15).

That phrase "rightly dividing" could also be translated "cutting it straight." It was a reference to the exactness demanded by such trades as carpentry, masonry, as well as Paul's trade of tent-making. It conveys the idea of correctly and accurately using Scripture.

It's exciting when someone asks you a question and you draw a complete blank, and then suddenly an appropriate Scripture (that you have taken the time to commit to memory) just pops into your mind, and you share it with that person. What you are sharing is so good, you want to take notes on yourself!

You wouldn't think of going into battle without knowing how your weapons worked. Nor would you want to build a house without knowing how your tools worked (especially your power tools!). And, of course, you couldn't expect to catch many fish without knowing how to effectively use your rod, hooks, lures, and bait.

So know your Bible.

This doesn't mean that you can't share until you've got whole books memorized or until you think you finally understand everything there is to know (none of us would ever be able to share our faith then!). As you share, however, keep learning, keep reading. If someone stumps you with a question, say that you'll go and find out. Learn how to find answers in God's Word. Work on memorizing. Those tools will be invaluable as you continue to share your faith in the sea of life.

SEVENTEEN
TEAMWORK TO BRING IN THE CATCH

When you are fishing and a fish is hooked, a friend should be standing by to net it—just like that other fisherman in Ohio who helped Larry Shaw bag his fifty-three-pound muskie. It's teamwork! Cooperation is a key to effectively sharing your faith.

Did you ever notice that Jesus sent his disciples out in pairs? One could preach while another could pray. I remember how, as a young believer, I wanted to learn to be more effective in sharing the gospel. One day I went out with two more mature and experienced Christians (or so I thought). They approached some person, and one of them made a statement about Christ. Then the other Christian said that he didn't really agree with that statement, and they began to argue with each other! The unbeliever was so disgusted with them that he just walked away while these two debated some fine point of theology.

Obviously, we don't want to do that.

Working as a team can be such a blessing because the person you are speaking to about Christ may ask you a question you can't answer, but your partner can (or vice versa). Perhaps more important, while one is speaking, the other can be praying. Without question, sharing the gospel is a spiritual battle, and we all have a part to play. Scripture says, "Neither he who plants is anything, nor he who waters, but God who gives the increase" (1 Corinthians 3:7).

A classic example of believers working together is the Gospel story of the four men who brought their crippled friend to Jesus (see Luke 5:17-26). The house in which the Lord was ministering was jammed with people, and they could not get in. But these faithful friends would not be deterred. They decided to lower their friend down in front of the Lord—through the roof! So they climbed up there with their makeshift gurney on ropes and began to dig their way through the tiled roof of the home where Jesus was speaking.

Imagine the scene if you will. There is Jesus in this dark little room, opening the truths of the kingdom of God, when suddenly clumps of dirt and pieces of tile fall to the floor. Dust starts dropping down, and a shaft of bright light bursts into the room. Then, down through a hole in the ceiling comes this crippled man, lying on his cot. He is slowly lowered until he lands right in front of Jesus.

You could understand if the Lord had been irritated by this interruption of his talk. Instead, Jesus was touched by this wonderful demonstration of faith in action, and he not only healed the man but forgave him of his sins as well.

You see, only one of those men working alone could not have presented his friend to Jesus like that. It would have been very difficult for two—even three. But when all four friends worked together, it resulted in a changed life.

Of course, there will be times when you're all on your own talking with a friend about your faith. But in a sense, you're not alone, because you will have (should have!) asked your believing friends to be praying for you. Then, when you can bring other believers into the picture to also be this person's friends or to answer this person's questions, you're using teamwork to help "catch another fish."

EIGHTEEN
BAITING THE HOOK

Today there are all types of sophisticated devices that harness the latest technology to detect schools of fish, utilizing radar, electronics, and depth finders. I heard about a special camera that an angler can now use to take a peek under the water and see where the fish are. Then there are thousands of lures you can choose from.

When we go fishing for men, we need to realize that what works for one doesn't necessarily work for another. Don't get me wrong. I'm not suggesting that the essential gospel is not the same for every person, for indeed it is. The bottom line, as I will point out later, is that very message. At the same time, however, we may initially approach different people with different "bait" to get their attention.

DIFFERENT BAIT FOR DIFFERENT FISH

For instance, if someone is strung out on drugs and/or alcohol, you might emphasize that only Jesus can fill the void that person has tried to fill with these substances. If you once struggled with these yourself, you could share your own personal story of how God filled the void in your life you once tried to fill with these cheap worldly imitations. If it is not your personal experience, you could mention the stories of some you probably know personally who came out of this kind of background and are now walking with the Lord.

If you are speaking to a person who is terminally ill or is on his or her deathbed, obviously the most important thing to that person is not so much filling a void in his or her life but preparing for eternity. You could share the great promises of Scripture concerning life beyond the grave when we put our complete faith and trust in Jesus Christ. And if you come upon a person who has gone from relationship to relationship, trying to fill a void for God with a man or a woman, you could speak of what it is to have a relationship with the living God who will never abandon or "dump" him or her.

Some people may offer a quick statement about the Lord to practically everyone they meet. That can be good to some degree, but it is far more effective to take the time to share the gospel with one person. Like Jesus, we need to recognize the specific needs of individuals. God wants us to be responsible "sharpshooters," not haphazard "machine gunners"!

You may not have noticed this yet, but the favorite subject of conversation for most people is *themselves*.

That is why I have found one of the best ways to share one's faith is to simply listen. That's right—*listen*. You could compare this type of evangelism to a visit to the doctor's office. The doctor starts by saying something like, "Tell me where it's hurting." He does this so he can make a proper diagnosis. Then, after carefully listening to the description of your pain or ailment, he will prescribe the appropriate medication or procedure.

In the same way, one of the best ways to begin sharing Christ with others is to ask them about themselves. Find out about their family and background. Ask them what their thoughts are on a number of subjects. When a person shares his or her ideas, however, you don't want to immediately start disagreeing with him or her. Saying something like, "You actually believe something as stupid as that? What an idiot!" or "Wrong again, Philistine!" will only put that person on the defensive.

Just listen. Take it in. Then your turn will come.

Try to build a bridge from a statement which that person has made. For all practical purposes, this is what Jesus did when he conversed with (not just spoke to) the woman at the well. He asked her questions. He drew her out. He listened. He responded. And a conversion took place that day, that changed the woman's life forever.

NINETEEN
COMMUNICATION IS CRITICAL

Jesus never dealt with any two people in exactly the same way. He varied his approach from person to person. He was, after all, the Master Communicator.

Central in his dealings with others was His compassion. This is especially seen in Jesus' encounter with the Samaritan woman at the well (John 4:3-42).

Scripture says that in spite of His busy schedule and all that he had to do, he "had to go through Samaria," no doubt knowing that there was a lonely, hurting woman who would be coming to a certain well in that region.

As He was waiting for her at the well, there she came, drawing water in the heat of the day. She was an outcast, known for her immoral life. She had gone from marriage to marriage, each one ending tragically in divorce. And when she met Jesus, she was living in an immoral relationship with a man.

If anyone had the right to get up on a soapbox and give her a strong sermon about sexual sin, it was Jesus! He knew everything about her. He could have addressed all of the sins that she had committed. But He didn't.

As they conversed a bit, she became somewhat flippant in her responses to him. Jesus could have retorted, "Repent, you adulteress!" Yet, it's interesting to note that He didn't do that. He saw behind the façade to what was really troubling this woman.

Instead of hammering her for her immoral lifestyle, he went to the root of her problem: she was empty and separated from God. Then, lovingly and tactfully, Jesus shared with her that he as God could fill the void in her life that she had previously tried to fill with men.

He essentially told her that if she drank from the "well" of relationships, she would thirst again. But if she drank from his well of living water, she would never thirst again. She accepted Jesus that day, and immediately became a witness. Jesus stayed in that town for two days and many people believed—largely because this woman told them about Jesus.

How different Jesus' approach to that woman is from many well-meaning but poorly trained Christians today. They act as though they are robots, spouting the same clichés to each person they meet without recognizing each individual's need. It's important to know whom you're speaking to, and how best to grab their attention.

KNOW YOUR AUDIENCE

This was the very strategy Paul used when he spoke to the people at Mars Hill in Athens (see Acts 17:16-34).

Athens was the cultural and intellectual center of the world at that time. But as Paul walked the streets of this magnificent city with its incredible architecture and gleaming monuments, he was troubled. Everywhere he looked, there stood a statue, an altar, a temple, or a shrine to some god. They were made out of stone, brass, and even gold, silver, ivory, and marble—beautiful works of art, but idols nonetheless.

The city was overrun with idols. In fact, it was said in that day that it was easier to find a god in Athens than a person. Paul thought and prayed carefully about what he would say to these Athenians when he appeared before them. He could have understandably delivered a searing sermon on idolatry and false worship.

But Paul saw what was behind it all.

These people were largely ignorant. They really didn't know any better. So he stood before them and said, "Men of Athens, I notice that you are very religious, for as I was walking along I saw your many altars. And one of them had this inscription on it—'To an Unknown God.' You have been worshiping him without knowing who he is, and now I wish to tell you about him" (Acts 17:22-23, NLT).

What a perfect opening statement! Talk about building bridges. At that moment, I'm sure that the Athenians were really listening.

AVOID ARGUMENTS

Another practical tip: Don't be drawn into an argument. Scripture reminds us:

> Don't have anything to do with foolish and stupid arguments, because you know they produce quarrels. And the Lord's servant must not quarrel; instead, he must be kind to everyone, able to teach, not resentful. Those who oppose him he must gently instruct, in the hope that God will grant them repentance leading them to a knowledge of the truth, and that they will come to their senses and escape from the trap of the devil, who has taken them captive to do his will. (2 Timothy 2:23-26, NIV)

The woman at the well tried to draw Jesus into an argument about the religious and cultural differences between Samaritans and Jews.

Instead of entering into a fruitless discussion, Jesus brought her back to the main message.

No one has ever been argued into the kingdom of God.

There is a place for disagreement and for clearly making your point. At the same time, however, we must be careful not to lose sight of our objective. The goal is not to win an argument, but to win a person to Christ.

USE TACT

We need to utilize something that is sorely lacking in the evangelism toolbox of many believers today.

It's called tact.

Tact is essentially putting yourself in the other person's shoes. It is an intuitive perception of what to say and when to say it. We don't need to unnecessarily alienate the person to whom we are speaking.

I read about a barber who, as a young Christian, attended a meeting one night where the speaker stressed the need to share the gospel with others. The barber knew he was lacking in this area, so he determined that he would speak to the first person who sat in his chair for a haircut the next day.

The next morning, after the customer had been seated and the apron was tucked around his neck, the barber began to strop his razor vigorously. Testing the edge, he turned to the man in the chair and blurted out, "Friend, are you ready to die and meet God?"

The man looked at the razor and fled out the door—apron and all! The barber had the right idea. He just needed to use a little tact.

Going back to Philip, that evangelist displayed his tact brilliantly as he shared the gospel with the searching man from Ethiopia. As that man read aloud from Isaiah's book, Philip came up alongside him and asked, "Do you understand what you are reading?" (Acts 8:30, NLT).

Now that is friendly, bridge-building stuff. He didn't huff, "Hey, you! Yeah, you, you pagan! Did you know that you're going to hell?"

Instead, he sought to reach out to this man. And the Ethiopian responded in kind: "How can I [understand this], when there is no one to instruct me?" (Acts 8:31, NLT).

Then he invited Philip into his chariot to do just that. The result, once again, was a conversion.

Paul summed it up this way:

> When I am with the Jews, I become one of them so that I can bring them to Christ. When I am with those who follow the Jewish laws, I do the same, even though I am not subject to the law, so that I can bring them to Christ. When I am with the Gentiles who don't have the Jewish law, I fit in with them as much as I can. In this way, I gain their confidence and bring them to Christ…. Yes, I try to find common ground with everyone so that I might bring them to Christ. I do all this to spread the Good News, and in doing so I enjoy its blessings. (1 Corinthians 9:20-23, NLT).

Pray for God to give you sensitivity to whomever you speak about your faith. If you know them well, key in on their needs. If you don't, be sensitive and listen. You'll learn what is keeping them from the faith, and what you might be able to say to help. Don't argue, be tactful. You'll listen, and then you'll find that they will listen to you as well.

A STORY WORTH TELLING
TELL YOUR OWN STORY

One of the best ways to "build a bridge" to someone who does not have a relationship with Christ is through your personal testimony. This is basically your story of how you came to Jesus Christ. The wonderful thing about your testimony is that even if you are relatively young in the faith, you can still share about what God has done for you personally.

Consider the blind man who was miraculously healed by Jesus.

He was being cross-examined by the religious authorities on the fine points of theology when he gave this classic response: "One thing I do know. I was blind but now I see!" (John 9:25, NIV).

Let me tell you, that explanation is a lot more than most people in this world know today. Though a person may disagree with what you believe, they cannot deny what actually happened to you. You can tell him or her of your life and attitude before coming to Christ, then explain the changes that came afterward.

When an unbeliever sees that you can relate to his or her own life, he or she may be more open to what you have to say. In a way, it's like preaching directly to him or her without really doing so in so many words.

You might say something like, "I heard this Christian say that I needed to give my life to Christ. My first inclination was, 'I am a good person. I don't really need Jesus. That's for weak people.' But then that Christian said…." And you could go on from there to explain that person's response to your excuses.

In doing this, you're putting yourself in the other person's shoes.

NO STORY LIKE YOURS

It's interesting to note how often the apostle Paul used his personal testimony when sharing the gospel. You would think that this man of brilliant intellect, trained in the great knowledge of his day and possessing a tremendous grasp and understanding of Scripture, would lean upon his extensive knowledge and oratorical skills when telling others of the gospel. Yet more often than not, when standing before Roman governors and leaders, Paul would begin by telling his personal story of how he came to know Jesus Christ as his Savior and Lord.

Every believer has a testimony. Granted, some may be more dramatic than others, yet there is someone out there who is just like you. I mentioned earlier that if you had personally struggled with something, such as drugs or alcohol, before you were a Christian, you could share that fact as you show how God can fill the void in your life that you had previously tried to fill with substances.

You may say, "But Greg, I didn't come from a background like that at all. In fact, I've lived a relatively upright, moral life." Perhaps you tried to be as considerate and caring as possible. You were even somewhat religious. But there was still something missing in your life. One day, you discovered that "something" was Someone. You needed Jesus, and you came to put your faith in Him. You realized that no matter how good you were, you weren't quite good enough!

Don't you realize that is a powerful testimony? It's just as valid as the story of someone who has come out of a life of crime, gangs, or drugs. It's just different.

When you get down to the bottom line, we all essentially have the same testimony. We were all separated from God by sin. We all crossed that line deliberately and repeatedly. We all needed a Savior. Whether we were a down-and-outer or an up-and-outer, we were still out! But then Jesus came in.

DON'T EXAGGERATE OR GLORIFY THE PAST

Sometimes there is a temptation to exaggerate just how bad we were or make things sound a little bit worse than they were.

Avoid that temptation.

Always be truthful and honest when relating your story. I have heard some Christians share their personal testimonies, and they seem to get a bit more dramatic with each telling.

One other thing I would add about sharing your personal story: never focus on what you "gave up for God," but rather on what God gave up for you! For instance, some people will vividly describe the "old days" before they knew the Lord with such excitement and passion that it will sound like their old lives were better than their new ones. Or they may speak of the great sacrifices they made to follow Jesus. "I had it all in my old life," they may boast. "Women, parties, fun, success, money—you name it, I had it!" Then with a somber look on their faces and tears in their eyes, they intone, "But I am here to tell you I gave it all up for Jesus. Hallelujah!"

Oh, please. What did you really give up? You gave up emptiness, an ever-present guilt, a constant fear of death, and a certain judgment that was to follow. What did God give you in its place? He gave you fulfillment, forgiveness, and the hope of life beyond the grave. He sent His own dear Son to lay His life down for you at the cross of Calvary.

MAKE A BEELINE TO THE CROSS

I already mentioned how Paul often used his personal testimony of how he came to Christ. Still, he always made a "beeline to the cross." In other words, he always came back to the message of Jesus Christ's death and resurrection.

Paul wrote, "When I came to you, brothers, I did not come with eloquence or superior wisdom as I proclaimed to you the testimony about God. For I resolved to know nothing while I was with you except Jesus Christ and him crucified" (1 Corinthians 2:1-2, NIV).

What exactly is this gospel message we are to proclaim to this lost world? Paul gives a simple summation of the gospel in 1 Corinthians 15:1-4 (NIV):

> Now, brothers, I want to remind you of the gospel I preached to you, which you received and on which you have taken your stand. By this gospel you are saved, if you hold firmly to the word I preached to you. Otherwise, you have believed in vain. For what I received I passed on to you as of first importance: that Christ died for our sins according to the Scriptures, that he was buried, that he was raised on the third day according to the Scriptures.

Embed that thought deep into your mind. *The gospel in a nutshell is that Christ died for our sins, was buried, and was raised on the third day.* There are other elements I could mention, but that is the cornerstone—the death and resurrection of Jesus Christ.

Someone once asked C. H. Spurgeon if he could summarize his

Christian faith in a few words. He replied, "It is all in four words: Jesus died for me."

AN EMBARRASSING PERSONAL EXPERIENCE

I had an experience as a very young Christian that showed me early on the importance of knowing the Scriptures, for I was unprepared and, as a result, shamed.

The incident took place not long after I had the privilege of leading to the Lord that lady I mentioned at the beginning of this book. I was out on the streets of Newport Beach looking for more people to share the gospel with.

Allow me to backtrack for a moment. I had a friend I had known since early childhood named Gregg. Soon after I had accepted the Lord into my life, I ran into Gregg and told him of my decision. Seeing the look of concern on his face, I reassured him by saying, "Don't worry now, Gregg. I am not going to become one of those religious fanatics walking around with a Bible and a cross around my neck, saying, 'Praise the Lord!' I'm going to do this on my terms."

Gregg seemed satisfied with my reassurance. I had not seen him for a couple of weeks, and my passion for sharing the gospel had grown quite a bit after leading that lady to Christ. As I was walking down the street in Newport Beach, whom do I see walking toward me but Gregg. In my hand was a Bible, and around my neck—you guessed it—was a cross. Before I could catch myself, I blurted out to Gregg, "Praise the Lord!"

We both had a good laugh. He couldn't believe his eyes. I said, "Gregg, I know this looks crazy, but because Jesus is so real and has changed my life so much, I'm out here on the beach, telling people about Him!"

He was listening.

I thought to myself, What if my friend Gregg became a Christian? So I began to share with him what Christ said and how to know Him. He seemed interested. I continued on, excited with the possibility of his coming to Christ, when suddenly someone interrupted us. It was some guy who had been eavesdropping on our conversation.

"So you're a Christian?" he barked.

I eagerly said I was.

"Well, Christian," he challenged, "I have a few questions for you!"

I thought to myself, *Fire away! I'm already two weeks old in the Lord. I'm ready for anything!*

Then this fellow fired off about four or five hard questions in rapid succession—and I didn't have a clue about how to answer them.

Gregg joined in, "Yeah, Laurie. What about all that?"

I was speechless and embarrassed. "I really don't know the answers, guys," I said sheepishly. They both walked away, and I felt as though I had failed God.

That experience, however, was something of a watershed for me. It made me search the Scriptures. The Bible tells us in 1 Peter 3:15, "Always be ready to give a defense to everyone who asks you a reason for the hope that is in you, with meekness and fear."

There really wasn't anything wrong with my not knowing the answers to those particular questions; even people who have been believers for many years still don't have answers to some questions, because some things just require faith. However, I needed to be willing to answer these guys with a confident "I don't know, but I'll find out for you."

They were trying to divert me—and I let them do it. That day, I learned that I needed to prepare myself for those kinds of situations. And you should do the same. As you prepare and practice, you will develop the skill of seeing through the diversions and getting back to your story of what Jesus did for you—the story that only you can tell.

TWENTY
THE CORNERSTONES OF THE GOSPEL

The gospel!

We hear that phrase tossed around a lot today. We call a certain style of music "gospel music," designated as such because of a certain sound it has. When we really want someone to believe what we're saying, we might add, "Listen—this is the 'gospel truth'!"

Sadly, however, the word gospel has largely lost its meaning in today's culture. It is my personal opinion that most Americans—much less the rest of the world—haven't really heard a true gospel presentation.

We hear some people say that they are "preaching the gospel," when in reality they don't even seem to know what that term really means. For that matter, I think there may be a surprising number of people in the church itself who don't actually know what the gospel message really is. According to one survey, 75 percent don't even know what John 3:16 says!

What is the gospel? What elements must be in it for it to be accurate? Are there false gospels we must be aware of? You might say, "I'll leave that to you preachers and theologians to figure out. All I know is I'm already saved and going to heaven!"

But wait! We all need to know what the gospel is for two very important reasons: (1) We want to make sure that we have heard the true gospel and have responded to it, lest we have a false hope concerning a salvation we think we have; and (2) Jesus told us to "go into all the world and preach the gospel" (Mark 16:15)!

Those words aren't merely addressed to pastors, teachers, evangelists, and missionaries; they are addressed to every follower of Jesus Christ! We can't be disengaged or disinterested in this subject, for people's eternal destinies literally hang in the balance.

What would you think of a surgeon who just started cutting away at a patient without really knowing what he was doing? One mistake, and that person could be disabled for life or could even die on the operating table. Yet this message we bring has even more far-reaching consequences than that—for there are eternal ramifications. Still, so many are sloppy in this area.

GOOD NEWS, BAD NEWS

What elements must be present for the gospel to be the gospel? A technical definition of the word gospel is "good news."

We've all heard the expression "I have some good news and some bad news…." Upon hearing a statement like that, we usually want to know the worst first.

You may have heard about the doctor who said to his patient, "I have some good news and some bad news."

The patient replied, "What's the good news?"

The doctor said, "You only have three weeks to live."

Exasperated, the patient replied, "If that's the good news, what's the bad news?"

The doctor answered, "I should have told you two weeks ago!"

When it comes to the gospel, the bad news is the fact that we all stand as sinners before a holy God. No matter who we are, we have all sinned—sometimes in ignorance but more often on purpose. Yet even as a jeweler will display a beautiful ring or necklace against a dark velvet background to accentuate its beauty, God has chosen to show us just how good the Good News is by first telling us the bad news.

Once we see our complete weakness, our inability to do anything whatsoever to alleviate our wretched condition, we can better appreciate the ultimate gift God has given us:

> When we were still without strength, in due time Christ died for the ungodly. For scarcely for a righteous man will one die; yet perhaps for a good man someone would even dare to die. But God demonstrates His own love toward us, in that while we were still sinners, Christ died for us. (Romans 5:6-8).

Ponder that a moment.

Consider the beauty of salvation against the dark background of our sin. God didn't give us this gift because we in any way deserved it; He gave it to us because we were so undeserving. There was no other way to satisfy the righteous demands of God; we were utterly incapable of improving ourselves (much less save ourselves), and we faced a future in hell because of our sin.

Yet God, in His great love, sent his own Son to come down from heaven and die on the cross in our place. I love the way Paul personalized it when he said, "Christ…loved me and gave Himself for me" (Galatians 2:20).

A GAP ONLY GOD COULD BRIDGE

There was no other way to resolve this serious sin issue we all face. We know that God is perfect. And we know that man is imperfect and sinful. So Jesus, the God-man, was uniquely qualified to bridge the gap between sinful humanity and a holy God. He was the only one who could ever do that: "All this is from God, who reconciled us to himself through Christ and gave us the ministry of reconciliation: that God was reconciling the world to himself in Christ, not counting men's sins against them. And he has committed to us the message of reconciliation" (2 Corinthians 5:18-19, NIV).

It's not about what I did to please or reach God. I did everything to displease and fail to reach Him. As this passage says, "All this is from God, who reconciled us to himself through Christ."

This is why Jesus Christ is the only way to the Father! In fact, he said so Himself in John 14:6 (NIV): "I am the way, the truth, and the life. No one comes to the Father except through me."

In these politically correct times in which we are living, it is tempting to soft-pedal this issue and say something along the lines of "We all worship the same God. You can choose your path. I've chosen mine. Mine is Christ. But if you want to worship some other way, that's fine."

But it's not fine. Not at all. The book of Proverbs clearly tells us that "There is a way that seems right to a man, but its end is the way of death" (Proverbs 14:12).

The apostle Peter underscores this important fact, echoing Christ's words: "There is salvation in no one else! There is no other name in all of heaven for people to call on to save them" (Acts 4:12, NLT). Paul said the same thing: "There is one God and one mediator between God and men, the man Christ Jesus" (1 Timothy 2:5, NIV).

Jesus, being God, was the only one who could bridge the gap and shed His blood in our place. For we as Christians to say anything else is not only wrong—it is a misrepresentation of the gospel!

There, on that cross, all the sin of the world was poured upon Jesus Christ as he became the sin sacrifice for us: "He made Him who knew no sin to be sin for us, that we might become the righteousness of God in Him" (2 Corinthians 5:21).

The fact is, if humankind could have reached God any other way, Jesus would not have had to die. His voluntary death on the cross clearly illustrates the fact that there is no other way. Those who reject His loving offer of forgiveness—which is extended to all—do so at their own peril.

IT'S A DONE DEAL

That is why Jesus cried out these three words on the cross of Calvary: "It is finished" (John 19:30). That phrase can be translated many ways: "It is made an end of; it is paid; it is performed; it is accomplished!"

What was made an end of? Our sins—and the guilt that accompanied them. What was paid? The price of redemption! What was performed? The righteous requirements of the law! What was accomplished? The work the Father had given Jesus to do.

Finished was Satan's stronghold on humanity:

> [Jesus] wiped out the handwriting of requirements that was against us, which was contrary to us. And He has taken it out of the way, having nailed it to the cross. Having disarmed principalities and powers, He made a public spectacle of them, triumphing over them in it. (Colossians 2:14-15)

SIMPLE, BUT POWERFUL

In the book of Romans, Paul refers to the explosive power of the gospel: "I am not ashamed of the gospel of Christ, for it is the power of God to salvation for everyone who believes" (Romans 1:16).

That is a profound statement coming from such an intelligent, gifted communicator as Paul. If anyone could have talked people into becoming Christians by mere mental skills, it would have been Paul. Yet it is amazing to read the accounts in the book of Acts as he stood before government leaders, the rich, and the powerful and shared the simple message of Jesus' dying on the cross.

Paul is reminding us that there is power in the simple message of the life, words, death, and resurrection of Jesus Christ. We often underestimate the raw power the gospel has in reaching even the most hardened heart. Don't underestimate its appeal. Don't be ashamed of its simplicity. Don't add to it or take away from it. Just proclaim it—then stand back and watch what God will do.

I have been amazed time and time again at how God so powerfully uses this simple yet incredibly profound message to radically change lives. I have seen it transform hardened Satanists as well as devoutly religious people who had previously not understood their need for Christ. I have witnessed its ability to heal broken families, break people's addictions to drugs, and free individuals who have been deceived by various cults.

The gospel of Christ is the most powerful message ever given, and through it God can and does change even the most broken of lives.

TWENTY-ONE
BEWARE OF IMITATIONS

BEWARE OF A WATERED-DOWN GOSPEL THAT HAS NO "TEETH"

To "water down" the gospel means to speak of God's forgiveness without any mention of repentance or to present Jesus Christ as though He were some mere "additive" to make one's life a little better. It would be like saying, "All you have to do is ask Him in, and your life will be better, your clothes cleaner, and your teeth whiter!" This is obviously an exaggeration, but it's not too far from what some people are saying as you might think.

We must not leave out the important aspects of repentance and obedience. I've already pointed out that we can appeal to the emptiness and voids in people's lives, especially as we begin our time of sharing the gospel with them. At the same time, however, we must get down to brass tacks.

BEWARE OF A RULE-LADEN OR OVERLY COMPLEX GOSPEL THAT STRIPS THE MESSAGE OF ITS SIMPLICITY AND POWER

This would involve telling people that first they have to be baptized before they can become Christians, or that they must dress a certain way to be forgiven, etc. This is essentially adding works to a salvation that Scripture reminds us is "a gift from God" and is not "a reward for the good things we have done" (Ephesians 2:8-9, NLT).

Again, this is why Scripture reminds us that we as Christians should be "rightly dividing the word of truth" (2 Timothy 2:15). So read this section very carefully. As Scripture advises us, "Watch your life and doctrine closely. Persevere in them, because if you do, you will save both yourself and your hearers" (1 Timothy 4:16, NIV).

We must know what the Bible teaches. We must know what we believe. We must be careful to present the gospel accurately, making sure that certain key elements are in place. Why? Because there is a counterfeit gospel out there.

BEWARE OF A FALSE GOSPEL

Make no mistake about it. The devil is a master manipulator and imitator. One of the greatest tactics he has used with tremendous effect over the centuries is to imitate something—to offer a counterfeit version of it that is close enough to be believable to some but far enough away from the truth to actually damage the person who believes it.

Paul writes to the Galatians:

> I am astonished that you are so quickly deserting the one who called you by the grace of Christ and are turning to a different gospel—which is really no gospel at all. Evidently some people are throwing you into confusion and are trying to pervert the gospel of Christ. But even if we or an angel from heaven should preach a gospel other

than the one we preached to you, let him be eternally condemned! (Galatians 1:6-8, NIV)

Today, there are many new TV programs and movies coming out of Hollywood that deal with spiritual themes. They underscore such things as faith, life after death, the meaning of life, and more. The problem that I have observed with most of them is that their message is lopsided. It's a "Hollywood feel good" belief that could potentially give a person false assurance.

I recently watched a TV program along these lines that emphasized the theme "God is love." While that certainly is a biblical and important message (one that I repeatedly emphasize myself), we don't want to lose sight of the fact that this God of love is also a God of justice, holiness, and perfection. Moreover, we don't want to forget to point out that God showed this love to us by sending his only Son to die on the cross for our sins. And the only way to come to know this God of love is through Christ.

BEWARE OF IMITATIONS

This "false gospel" Paul warns us against says that all we have to do is believe—but it doesn't say that we need to *repent*. It speaks of heaven but leaves out the message of hell. On the other hand, it can be so complex that no one can unravel it, or it can come laden with rules and regulations that one must keep to find forgiveness. That's not very "good news."

General William Booth, founder of the Salvation Army, wrote of the dangers he saw that faced the message of the gospel in the twentieth century (and, I might add, the twenty-first century, too). Among other things, he saw a "gospel" that would present:

- Christianity without Christ
- Forgiveness without repentance
- Salvation without regeneration
- Heaven without hell

While this watered-down gospel is a real problem, so also is a gospel that would only warn of judgment and not offer God's gracious forgiveness. This is another important reason for you to know God's Word. Ask God to guide you as you study. Pray for discernment in order to know a false gospel when you hear it.

Be ready with the truth. People are longing for it!

TWENTY-TWO
THE STEPS TO THE DECISION

Suppose that the person you have been sharing the gospel with seems ready to receive Christ. You ask, "Is there any good reason why you shouldn't accept Jesus Christ right now?"

Much to your shock, they say, "No. I want to accept Christ right now!"

What then? I like to make sure that person fully understands what he or she is doing. I often make five points at the end of my evangelistic messages. They were adapted from a message by Billy Graham at Madison Square Garden in the 1950s.

Here they are:

ONE: REALIZE THAT YOU ARE A SINNER.

This is a hard one for people to admit. Yet Romans 3:23 clearly says,

"All have sinned and fall short of the glory of God." We must first accept full responsibility for our sins.

TWO: RECOGNIZE THAT JESUS CHRIST DIED FOR YOUR SINS.

Because there was no other way to resolve this problem of our sin, God sent his own Son to die in our place on the cross of Calvary. Romans 5:8 says, "While we were still sinners, Christ died for us." Jesus said, "God so loved the world that He gave His only begotten Son, that whoever believes in Him should not perish but have everlasting life" (John 3:16).

THREE: YOU MUST REPENT.

Acts 17:30 (NIV) says, "God…commands all people everywhere to repent." To repent means that you have been going the wrong way in life, and you need to start going God's way. Instead of running from God, you run to Him.

FOUR: YOU MUST RECEIVE JESUS CHRIST INTO YOUR LIFE.

Jesus said, "Behold, I stand at the door and knock. If anyone hears My voice and opens the door, I will come in" (Revelation 3:20). Being a Christian is not merely believing a creed or even going to a church. You can do those things and not necessarily have your sin forgiven and have Christ in your heart. There must come a moment in every person's life where he or she says, "Lord, come in."

Scripture tells us, "To all who believed him and accepted him, he gave the right to become children of God" (John 1:12, NLT).

FIVE: YOU MUST DO IT NOW!

Second Corinthians 6:2 (NLT) says, "Today is the day of salvation." This could be the person's last opportunity to respond to the gospel.

TWENTY-THREE
A DECISION DEFERRED IS NO DECISION

Let's say that the person you have been sharing with is ready right then and there to make that commitment. Then I strongly urge you, if possible, to find a quiet place and to lead the person in a prayer of receiving Christ. Don't tell him or her to think it over and get back to you. Seize the moment!

Why is it so important to do it right then? The story is told of the great evangelist, D. L. Moody, who preached an evangelistic message one night in Chicago. He decided to give his listeners a night to think over the question "What will you do with Jesus?"

Then he asked them to consider coming back the next evening to hear him preach again. The next morning Chicago lay in ashes. On October 8, 1871, the very night of his message, the Great Chicago Fire started. Many who were in his audience died in that blaze.

To his dying day, Moody regretted that he had told the people to wait. He never forgot that hard-learned lesson. He later wrote:

> I have never dared to give an audience a week to think of their salvation since. If they were lost they would rise up in judgment against me. I want to tell one lesson I learned that night which I have never forgotten, and that is when I preach, to press Christ upon the people then and there, and try to bring them to a decision on the spot. I would rather have my right hand cut off than to give an audience a week now to decide what to do with Jesus.

TWENTY-FOUR
THE REASONS PEOPLE SAY NO

Many of us know what it is like to be sharing the gospel with someone and suddenly find ourselves barraged by an endless stream of questions and so-called "reasons" as to why the person has not trusted Christ as Savior.

I believe that most of these are not honest questions or reasons as much as they are excuses. And you know what an excuse is, don't you?

It's just a fancy lie.

Excuses have been defined as "the skin of a reason stuffed with a lie." An excuse is what we offer up when we really don't want to do something. Many will hide behind excuses because they really don't want to come to Christ. And the reason they don't want to come to

Christ is that they really don't want to change.

Let me first address four of the most commonly asked questions about the Christian faith:

ONE: IF GOD IS SO GOOD AND LOVING, WHY DOES HE ALLOW EVIL?

This one is always on the top of people's lists of questions about God! We are asked, "Why does He allow babies to be born blind, or war, or injustice, or tragedy?" In the classic statement of the problem, either God is all-powerful but not all good; therefore, He doesn't stop evil. Or He is all good but not all-powerful; therefore, He can't stop evil.

The general tendency is to blame God for evil and suffering, passing all responsibility on to him. However, God is getting a bad rap! You see, people were created with the ability to choose. We have the freedom to choose to love or not to love, to do right or to do wrong, to obey or disobey.

In the Garden of Eden, those first people made the wrong choice, and sin entered into the world: "Sin entered the world through one man, and death through sin, and in this way death came to all men, because all sinned" (Romans 5:12, NIV).

As a result, we live in a world that is fallen and imperfect. Because sin entered the world through Adam, the entire planet has been affected. The curse came not only on humanity, but on all creation as well. The repercussion of that was the entrance of sin into the world. And with that sin came many problems, like sickness and even death.

Up to that point, men and women would have lived forever in their perfect bodies. But now this body of ours wears out and breaks down with the passing of time. Disease, sickness, disabilities—all came as a result of the curse of sin. They are not a punishment for a sin that we have committed, but rather are the result of sin in general.

The point that we must keep in mind is that man—not God—is responsible for sin! Take wars, for instance. They are not initiated by God, but by humanity. The apostle James tells us where they come from: "What is causing the quarrels [wars] and fights among you? Isn't it the whole army of evil desires at war within you? You want what you don't have, so you scheme and kill to get it. You are jealous for what others have, and you can't possess it, so you fight and quarrel to take it away from them" (James 4:1-2, NLT).

Yet, in spite of our wrong choices, God intervenes. He is able and willing to forgive us, even when we have horribly sinned. The Bible says, "If we confess our sins, He is faithful and just to forgive us our sins and to cleanse us from all unrighteousness" (1 John 1:9). God can even use something like sickness to bring us to Himself. God can speak to us through tragedy or hardship. C. S. Lewis wrote, "God whispers to us in our pleasures, speaks in our conscience, but shouts in our pains; it is his megaphone to arouse a deaf world."

Sadly, God has to use his "megaphone" for some of us. It's the only thing that will get our attention. The psalmist writes, "Before I was afflicted I went astray, but now I keep Your word" (Psalm 119:67).

As Christians, however, we have the hope that one day "God will wipe away every tear from their eyes; there shall be no more death, nor sorrow, nor crying. There shall be no more pain, for the former things have passed away" (Revelation 21:4). You can point out to the person asking this question that only Christians have that hope. Then ask him or her, "Do you?"

TWO: HOW CAN YOU CHRISTIANS SAY THAT JESUS IS THE ONLY WAY? DON'T ALL ROADS LEAD ULTIMATELY TO GOD?

This particular cornerstone of the Christian faith is especially irritating to many unbelievers in these pluralistic times. They may get in your face and shout, "Are you saying that Jesus Christ is the only way and that if someone does not believe in Him, they are actually going to hell?"

Then they proceed to label you as "narrow," "bigoted," "insensitive," and (probably the worst thing that you can be accused of in this day and age) "intolerant."

To such people, it may sound as though you are implying that you are somehow better than they are or that you look down on them because of your belief in Christ. Yet you need to let them know that the reason you believe that Jesus Christ is the only way to the Father is quite simply because He said so Himself. As I quoted earlier, Jesus tells us in Scripture, "I am the way, the truth, and the life. No one comes to the Father except through Me" (John 14:6).

If I claim to be His follower and believe His words, then I would be less than honest if I said anything but this. As a Christian, I am most certainly not better than or superior to anyone else. I'm just one beggar telling another beggar where to find food.

Someone may say, "If a person is really sincere in what he or she believes, he or she will get to heaven." This type of fuzzy, illogical thinking is typical of so many today, causing them to make the most important decisions of life on the basis of their personal thoughts and feelings. It's as though they were somehow the "moral center of the universe."

Do you really think sincerity is enough?

Take this line of reasoning to its logical conclusion. If a person truly is sincere in what he or she believes and tries to live a good life, then he or she will get to heaven. So Adolf Hitler is in heaven, right? He sincerely believed that what he was doing was right. Charles Manson is okay, too, right? And what about Jim Jones?

The person may protest, "No! They weren't good!" But according to whose definition? Yours? Mine? The person's next door? Is it determined by consensus? Why is it wrong to lie, steal, and murder? Who says? It comes back to the fact that we have to have a set of absolutes we live by. We can't simply make up the rules as we go.

Many want to believe that all roads lead to God and that every religion is basically true. We would like to think that all religions blend beautifully together, but they really don't. You see, only Jesus Christ was both God and man. Only Jesus was qualified to bridge the way to a holy God. The Bible says, "There is one God and one Mediator between God and men, the Man Christ Jesus" (1 Timothy 2:5).

Jesus also said, "He who is not with Me is against Me" (Luke 11:23). Jesus does not say, "Admire me," He says, "Follow me!"

And that is the decision each person must make.

THREE: HOW CAN A GOD OF LOVE SEND PEOPLE TO HELL?

In the first place, God doesn't send anyone to hell. People send themselves there. Hell was never created for people, it was created for the devil and his angels. When speaking of the destiny of those who hypocritically claimed to follow Him, Jesus said, "Depart from Me, you cursed, into the everlasting fire prepared for the devil and his angels" (Matthew 25:41).

The fact is, God doesn't want anyone to go to hell! In Ezekiel 33:11, God says, "I have no pleasure in the death of the wicked, but that the wicked turn from his way and live." Second Peter 3:9 reminds us, "The Lord is not…willing that any should perish, but that all should come to repentance."

Here's an illustration you could use in explaining this to an unbeliever. Let's say that you are driving on the freeway and are on your way to cross a large bridge over a raging river. Suddenly, you see a large sign that reads: *Warning! Bridge Out! Use Other Exit!* Nevertheless, you are determined, so you speed up toward that bridge. As you get closer, you see more signs: *Don't Enter! Danger! Bridge Out!* Still, you frantically speed on.

As you get really close, you see police cars with lights flashing and officers waving and yelling for you to turn back. Yet you continue on until you break through those barriers and drive off the top of the bridge, plunging to a watery grave.

Now whose fault would that be? It would be your own. You ignored the warnings. You were determined to do what you wanted to do in spite of the roadblocks that were erected for your own protection.

Know this: no one will be in hell or heaven by accident. That is why God sent Jesus—to provide us with God's gracious "roadblocks." If we reject them, the Bible asks, "How shall we escape if we neglect so great a salvation?" (Hebrews 2:3).

FOUR: THERE ARE TOO MANY HYPOCRITES IN CHURCH!

We've all heard people say, "The reason I am not a Christian is because there are too many hypocrites in the church! When I find the perfect, hypocrite-free church, then maybe I'll join."

All I can say is that if those people do find the perfect, "hypocrite-free" church, they shouldn't join it. They would only spoil it.

Sadly, there is a great deal of hypocrisy in the church today. You will find many people attending church who are pretending to be something they aren't. I heard the story of a man who was desperate to make some money, so he went down to the city zoo, hoping to get a job feeding the animals. The manager at the zoo had no openings, but seeing how big this man was, he offered him another possible position.

"Our gorilla died the other day, and that was one of our most popular exhibits! If we got you a special gorilla suit, would you put it on and imitate him for a few days? We'll pay you well for it!"

The guy was so desperate he agreed. He actually did quite well over the next few days. He would dress up in his gorilla suit, beat his chest, and shake the bars of his cage. Huge crowds soon gathered at the exhibit. And the money was good.

One day, however, while performing his gorilla act, he was swinging on his trapeze and accidentally lost his grip. This landed him right in the middle of the lion's den! The huge beast gave a ferocious roar. The man in the gorilla suit realized he couldn't cry for help without revealing that he was a fake.

He slowly walked backward away from the lion, hoping to climb back into his cage. The lion, with a very hungry look on his face, started to follow him. Finally in desperation the man in the gorilla suit cried out, "Help!"

Immediately the lion whispered loudly, "Shut up, stupid! You'll get us both fired!"

Unfortunately, like the "pseudo-zoo" in this story, you will find hypocrites in the church today. You can't deny that when confronted with this excuse. Yet you must also point out that just because someone attends a church does not necessarily mean that he or she is even a Christian! That hypocrite the unbeliever cites as an example may not even be a real follower of Jesus to start with.

Then again, there are those who are true believers who haven't lived the Christian life as they should. It might not be a bad idea if we Christians wore a sign around our neck that said, "Under Construction."

But I do know this: Jesus didn't say, "Follow My people"; He said, "Follow Me." He will never be a hypocrite. He will never be inconsistent. He will be all He promises to be in our life.

TWENTY-FIVE
THE REAL REASON PEOPLE SAY NO

What's the real reason people say no to Jesus, as opposed to the excuses? Jesus gave the answer in the third chapter of John's Gospel:

> "This is the verdict: Light has come into the world, but men loved darkness instead of light because their deeds were evil. Everyone who does evil hates the light, and won't come into the light for fear that his deeds will be exposed. But whoever lives by the truth comes into the light, so that it may be seen plainly that what he has done has been done through God" (John 3:19-21, NIV).

Many people simply don't want to change.
They want to continue as they always have.

They may point to this or that excuse, but the bottom line is that they don't really want to change. But we must not give up on them! I shared a story earlier in the book about the first person that I was able to lead to Christ. But I must tell you that I wasn't very bold about sharing my faith in the beginning.

A few days after I had received Christ on my high school campus, I was sort of in a spiritual no-man's land. I wasn't really comfortable with the Christians on campus yet, and I had not been back to see my old friends since I had made this commitment.

At lunchtime, I decided that I would go back and hang out with some of my old buddies, just for old times' sake. I certainly didn't want to tell them about my newfound faith. I wanted to keep it as quiet as possible.

One of my friends had a house right next to our campus, so we would often hang out there at lunchtime. As I was making my way there, one of the Christians on campus recognized me and yelled out (very loudly, I might add), "Hey, brother Greg! Praise the Lord!"

"Yeah, right—uh, praise the Lord," I muttered.

"Hey, bro," this zealous Christian said, "I've got something for you!" He then proceeded to hand me a rather large Bible with a faded leather cover. Glued on the front of it were two Popsicle sticks in the shape of a cross! To be honest with you, I really didn't want this Bible or this very public conversation with this outspoken Christian at that moment.

"Read it, and you will grow spiritually!" he promised.

"Uh, okay. Thanks. I'll do that," I sheepishly replied.

After he left, I thought to myself, *What am I going to do with this Bible? I can't actually carry it publicly across campus. People will think I'm some kind of religious nut!*

So being the bold witness for Christ that I was, I proceeded to take the Bible with its Popsicle sticks in the shape of a cross on it and stuff it into my coat pocket. Because of the sheer size of it, this caused my pocket to rip.

I slowly made my way over to my friend's house and was ready to walk in when I remembered the Bible in my coat pocket. I didn't want my friends to see Greg Laurie carrying Scripture around, so I looked for some place to ditch it. There in front of my friend's house was a planter. I quickly looked both ways, hid my Bible under some leaves, and made my way inside.

As I casually sauntered in, my friends seemed somewhat surprised to see me.

"Hey, Laurie, where ya been?"

"Nowhere," I said, as nonchalantly as I could.

"So whatcha been doing?"

"Nothing," I said.

One of them said, "Hey, you wanna smoke some weed [marijuana] before class?"

Now, to be perfectly honest, if they had asked me that same question a few days earlier, I might have said yes. But it suddenly just didn't seem right.

"No!" I said rather strongly, surprising even myself a little bit. All the time that this was going on, my heart was beating like a drum. It was as though I heard the Lord speaking to my heart saying, "Tell them about me." In response I was saying, "No! You tell them if you want to!"

Suddenly the front door burst open. There stood my friend's mother with my Bible in her hand—Popsicle sticks and all!

"Who does this belong to?" she demanded.

Every eye in the room looked at that Bible and then at me. Somehow they just knew there was a connection.

"It's mine," I said very quietly.

"What is that, Laurie?" one of my buddies shouted at me.

"It's a Bible," I said, again, very quietly.

"A *what*?" my buddies asked.

"A Bible! A B–I–B–L–E!"

One of them said very sarcastically, "Oh, praise the Lord, brother

Greg. Are we going to be good little Christians now and read the Bible and go to church?"

I shot back, "No! We're going to hit you in the mouth if you don't shut up!" (I hadn't yet read the part about loving your neighbor in the Bible I was hiding.)

Needless to say, I wasn't a very bold witness for Jesus Christ in the beginning. But it wasn't long until I realized that I could not, as a Christian, live in two worlds. Nor could I hide what God had so graciously done for me.

Becoming a Christian means changing—and some people are just plain scared!

KEEP TRYING

There is an old proverb that says, "When you throw a rock into a pack of dogs, the one that barks the loudest is the one that has been hit." Sometimes the people who are the most argumentative and combative may actually be closer to coming to Christ than you may think.

There may be one person you are sharing the gospel with who is very kind about it when you speak to him or her. He or she may say things like, "Oh, I'm so glad that you have found religion. You seem to be a lot happier than you used to be."

You might reply that it is not religion you have found, but a personal relationship with Jesus Christ.

You might ask that person to go to church with you, and he or she will sweetly say, "You know, I would really like to do that some time."

You may think to yourself, "This person is really close to coming to Christ." Maybe so, maybe not. Things are not always as they seem. There might be someone else who is always giving you a hard time about the gospel. Every Monday at work or school, they barrage you with a bunch of new questions they dreamed up for you over the weekend. They may scream and yell, creating a big scene. But remember, "When you throw a rock into a pack of dogs…."

In reality, the person who is so sweet and understanding when you share the gospel may be very far from the kingdom, while the person who is always creating a fuss, arguing, and generally giving you a hard time may be very close.

I recently had a conversation with a man who is now the leader of a Christian denomination. He told me of how he used to be this way. A faithful believer had been sharing with him for some time. This particular man would mock, cajole, harass, and deride this Christian day in, day out. But the Christian wouldn't give up. So one day, this man went to church just to get this Christian off his back.

The two men happened to come to a church where I was preaching, and when I shared a gospel message from the Word of God that day, the hostile man came to Christ. So don't give up!

STEP OUT

Today Jesus continues to say, "The harvest is plentiful but the workers are few. Ask the Lord of the harvest, therefore, to send out workers into his harvest field" (Matthew 9:37-38, NIV).

Notice that Jesus doesn't say to pray for more observers or more spectators or more complainers. He is asking that you pray for more laborers. But we can't honestly pray that prayer if we aren't willing to do it—to step out and be those laborers.

Unfortunately, it seems like the church today could be compared to a giant football game, with sixty thousand people in the stands watching while twenty-two people do all the work. We all stand on the sidelines and say, "Go, team! Go!"

But God is saying, "I want you down on the field. I want you to carry the ball. I want you to be a part of what I am doing."

You may feel unqualified for the calling, but think of what Jesus did with the twelve disciples. When we think of these men, we often think of them as holy or special. Yet though they were gifted and dedicated, they were ordinary. Jesus didn't call them because they were great. Their greatness was the result of the call of Jesus.

God wants to use you. He has a place for you, a part for you to play, a seed for you to sow, a call for you to answer, a fish for you to catch! Begin by asking God's Holy Spirit to stir your heart so that you can answer this desire and wish of Jesus.

You may pray something like this: "Lord, let it start with me. Make me a laborer—a fisher of men and women in this sea of life. I don't know what I can do. I feel a bit like that kid in the Bible who just had the loaves and fish. Here is my lunch, Lord—it's not much, but I give it to You."

If you pray that type of heartfelt prayer, just watch what God will do!

Leading people to Christ is the most joyful experience I know of next to having met him myself. I like the statement of C. H. Spurgeon, who said, "To be a soul winner is the happiest thing in this world. With every soul you bring to Jesus Christ you seem to get a whole new heaven on earth."

This is not a suggestion. This is not an option. It is a command. But it is a blessed command—and a tremendous privilege. So get out there, and start doing your part. Let's go fishing!

ENDNOTES

1   Walter A. Elwell and Philip W. Comfort, eds., *Tyndale Bible Dictionary* (Wheaton, Ill.: 2001), 169.

ALLEN DAVID BOOKS Other AllenDavid Books
Published by
Kerygma Publishing

KERYGMA PUBLISHING

Visit: www.kerygmapublishing.com
www.allendavidbooks.com
www.harvest.org